The Road Less Traveled

The Road Less Traveled

—— *Reclaiming Childhood for Christianity* ——

Kyle Townes

RESOURCE *Publications* · Eugene, Oregon

THE ROAD LESS TRAVELED
Reclaiming Childhood for Christianity

Resource Publications
An Imprint of Wipf and Stock Publishers
199 W. 8th Ave., Suite 3
Eugene, OR 97401

www.wipfandstock.com

PAPERBACK ISBN: 979-8-3852-5247-3
HARDCOVER ISBN: 979-8-3852-5248-0
EBOOK ISBN: 979-8-3852-5249-7

VERSION NUMBER 07/09/25

Contents

Acknowledgments

I COULD NEVER THANK sufficiently those in my life who have supported me through prayer, words, and action, and who therefore contributed in some way to this book. Beginning with my own parents, who have spent their lives in service and dedication to our entire family, thank you for your shining example of what parents should be. As I've told you since I was little, "I love you more than life!" I also want to thank my husband, who not only helped in every possible way while I was writing this book, but who also actively supports me on a daily basis. You are my best friend and my most kindred spirit. I love you.

To my beautiful children, who took over the house while I worked on this project and ran it like the little women they are, thank you. You are selfless, loving, and thoughtful, and most importantly of all, you believe in the Lord Jesus Christ for the forgiveness of all your sins. I am forever honored that God chose me to be your mother, and my life is full of meaning because you are in it.

Thank you to Joshua and Kristi Pauling, whose editing advice and insightful suggestions greatly helped me to improve this book. I am so grateful. Thank you also to Brannon Ellis, who, although we did not work on this book together, has in the past selflessly shared his wisdom on how to be a better writer and consistently encouraged me to keep writing. I will be forever grateful to you.

Preface

WHY WRITE THIS BOOK? There is no shortage of parenting books offering advice and encouragement for parents. I've been told that these books usually don't sell well, and I can understand why. The market is saturated with them. And what, after all, do they truly have to offer? Feel-good stories, the effects of which wear off after a few hours or a few days at most, leaving the reader with nothing more than what they started with. Empty words clutter the page, leaving only faint impressions of someone else's supposed peace and tranquility, with no meaningful direction provided for our own lives.

And don't get me started on Christian parenting books in particular! The lack of reliance on God's word to guide our decisions as parents is the hallmark of many of these books. Add to that the fact that concrete evidence, studies, and statistics are left by the wayside because we must exist in a realm of feelings as Christians, making our parenting decisions based on our emotions, and you've concocted the perfect poison. The hard truths—the necessary discussions—remain untouched in favor of more palatable and emotional topics. These books are good for the fire and nothing more, precisely because they lead many astray into modern ideologies of child-rearing under the guise of Christian wisdom, encouraging parents to make decisions based on a mere fantasy world instead of reality.

I wrote this book because, for many years, while raising my children, I have been acutely aware of the situation regarding Christian families in America and what is being said (or, more accurately, not being said) in response to it. Over the years, my dismay at this situation has continually grown.

There is a great divorce in our culture between what we believe as Christians and how we parent. Modern ideology has so deeply infiltrated the Christian family unit that if you place the average Christian family side by side with the average pagan family, you'll find them virtually indistinguishable. The way the children behave, talk, are disciplined, spend their free time, dress, treat their parents and other authorities, what they watch on their screens, how they value their education, and even their knowledge of Holy Scripture—all of it shows no real difference from their pagan counterparts. True, there is no intrinsic good that comes just from being different. That's not the goal. You don't gain anything just by standing out from the crowd. We should not impose a law where there is no law either, swinging the pendulum from one extreme to another, and establishing rules to demonstrate how unique and dissimilar we are from the world.

However, when it comes to daily living and childrearing, we find that we are not standing in purely neutral territory, as has long been the accepted idea. This is not an area of life where God has nothing to say and no opinion to give. The deeper we go into Christianity, the more we recognize the foolishness of that thought for any aspect of life! God is clear: what we see, hear, say, and do matters. It shapes and forms our character. And sin also matters. It seeks to pull us away from God, and we should walk cautiously and remain alert to it in our lives and in our children's lives. We should care about how everything molds and shapes us. Education can be seen as mental formation, teaching our children not only how they should think about the world but also about what is true and what is false, right and wrong, good and evil—in other words, about reality as a whole. Therefore, education also greatly matters.

For years, we traveled the country as a military family and met Christians from all walks of life and in various circumstances. During this time, I was continually struck by how unusual our family appeared to other Christians for reasons that should *not* make us stand out amongst believers. Our children were well behaved—that was seen as very odd. We were careful about what they put into their hearts and minds—that was certainly bizarre. We took sin in ourselves and our children seriously—another eye-raising notion. I couldn't understand why this was not a commonality amongst other Christian families. My heart would sink when I'd meet another believing family who viewed these matters as strange. After all, God seems to take sin seriously, and He seems to believe that what enters the eyes and ears impacts the heart. God has commanded that children be disciplined and learn self-control. He says that it is important. So why do I feel like a foreigner among my own people for caring about these things? I searched for someone else speaking the truth around me and for others who would call Christians to raise their children according to the Lord's clear direction and against societal notions contrary to His word. Someone. Anyone.

I found only silence.

I resisted the call to write this book for many years. I thought I wasn't up to the task. I am not a theologian or an important figure, and I haven't spent years climbing the corporate ladder in a lucrative career, so what do I have to offer? I also tend to be too blunt, which often doesn't go over well. I didn't feel articulate or smart enough to write a book. All these reasons combined to assure me that I could not be called to write about this. Someone else, better and more equipped than I, will eventually come along. They will be the one to write it. So, I watched and waited. But nothing changed that I could see, and the call persisted. The silence on these topics was deafening, at least from my vantage point.

Christianity places a high value on life and children, and by extension, also on education, which is the process of seeking truth. It provides a foundation and a structure from which all of life can be built. And that foundation is easily laid in early childhood. This structure naturally takes shape at a young age. Yet, we are squandering our children's youth; we are dulling their minds and handicapping their abilities, all because we are following the secular herd of sheep off the cliff.

So, despite my inabilities, I decided to write and leave the rest to God. As my dad says, "The Trinity doesn't have to hold a conference to figure this one out." I knew He would find a way to enable me to do this if this is what He wanted me to do.

This book aims to encourage parents with God's word, provide focus to the directionless, and help raise a generation of young believers rooted and connected to their faith, able to think logically and equipped to enter this hostile world. God help us all in our arduous and impactful calling as caretakers of these precious little ones made in God's image!

Introduction

I HAVE ALWAYS BEEN a fact-based person, especially when it comes to making important decisions. When a question falls into the "life-changing" category, I need direct, factual answers. Evidence is what I'm looking for when I choose between one path and another. If all I receive is personal opinion or subjective experience, I know that is not the path for me because those things change with the tide and vary from person to person. How can I make life-altering decisions based on something as flimsy as that? I need solid ground on which to stand. So, it must be facts, and the search is on to find out what reality is regarding the question at hand and, most importantly, to learn and understand if God has had anything to say about it.

Many parents out there feel the same way. They are looking for guidance in their parenting, but they feel completely lost. Something nags at them, suggesting there is a better way, yet they don't know what it is or how to find it. What should they look for when making their choices? They've been told that God has not spoken about this topic of childrearing, meaning that the first place they would normally start (the Bible) is apparently not an option. When they seek direction from others in their lives, they find everyone pointing them toward a different path. It starts to feel like they have to close their eyes and pick a random direction, like pin the tail on the donkey. All paths seem to lead up the same mountain, anyway. The indication is that whatever they do with their children doesn't matter, which is somewhat reassuring since they have no idea what they're doing. However, when looking at friends and family, they can clearly see that not all childrearing paths do, in fact, lead up the same mountain. The results of different parenting strategies could not be more dramatically different. This worldly perspective, viewing childrearing as a game of chance, has taken many Christian parents from feeling anxious to frustrated to lost, often culminating in a feeling of utter despair.

I wanted to write a book for parents who, like me, want more from a parenting book than just a nice life story, because they understand what is at stake. They desire to follow the Lord, and above all, they want their children to do the same. They aim to make wise decisions for their children based on what is objectively the best option for them. I'm here to tell you that some options are indeed better than others, and God has not been as silent as you might think regarding this vocation we have as parents.

In this life, parenting can be one of the loneliest and hardest jobs, even when you have a clear direction and know you are on the best path for your family. It can feel like our four walls are closing in on us, that nobody understands how hard we're working, how difficult our children are being, or how deeply we are struggling with our sinful nature (show of hands of who struggles with their patience, please?). It can seem like the doubts that assail us in the darkest moments are unique to us, and we may begin to believe we are incapable of fulfilling the job God has given us to do. We feel like failures while everyone around us appears better equipped. We think we cannot do it and need someone else to do it for us, whether that be a school or a screen. We want to give up.

If you feel that way, or I should say when you feel that way, I hope you'll pick up this book and find encouragement. I've certainly been there. All God-fearing parents have walked this path. As Christian moms and dads, we are, in fact, warriors for Christ—fighting the largest spiritual battles of our lives[1]—and God is equipping us and our children for the work He has given us to do. This calling is a huge task. A gargantuan responsibility. Raising up children in the Lord is no small feat. But Christ is with you. He will never fail you. You are not alone.

---

1. "For our struggle is not against flesh and blood, but against the rulers, against the authorities, against the powers of this dark world and against the spiritual forces of evil in the heavenly realms." Eph 6:12.

1

The Journey

MY NAME IS KYLE, which throws a lot of people off. "Is it . . . Kylie?" I usually tell them, "No, it's just Kyle . . . like a boy." Many people who haven't met me in person assume it's my husband's name. Let me explain: I'm from California. Usually that's enough explanation, but if you're unfamiliar with California culture, it's a *bit* off the beaten track. And by a bit, I mean a *lot*. We'll just say it's in our DNA to be different.

I grew up in Santa Barbara, a lovely coastal town a few hours north of Los Angeles. The mountains loomed right behind our house, giving Santa Barbara that small-town feel of being somewhat cut off from the rest of the world. We were not isolated by any means. Santa Barbara is the town of celebrities and millionaires who come from LA and hide away in a ritzy section known as Montecito. They flock to this little oasis because Santa Barbara boasts exquisite beauty. Large, old trees are everywhere, charming stucco buildings dot the area, and red-tiled roofs glisten in the sun. There is a quaint main street filled with numerous local restaurants, a gorgeous historic mission, several beaches, and, of course, California's fantastic weather. We didn't live in the ritzy part of Santa Barbara; we lived in a simple little house on a cul-de-sac up a steep hill, bordered by a large canyon on one side, but it was perfect. My dad was a hard-working lawyer, and my mom devoted herself to raising me and my older sister, a choice that had a lifelong impact on me.

Educational Experience

I have experienced nearly every type of mainstream educational system. I attended public school from kindergarten until the middle of third grade. I was pulled out of school in the middle of third grade because the school was so disordered that my parents could no longer ignore the problems there. In my mind, it was my constant pleas to be homeschooled that had finally paid off. The school environment had been completely chaotic, with teachers occupying class time with activities like playing cartoons and giving lengthy lessons on how to brush your teeth. I was getting headaches almost daily from the noise level in the classrooms as the kids were out of control. It was miserable. Unfortunately, that's about all I remember from my early days in public school.

I was homeschooled until high school and enjoyed it. I remember reading many excellent books and completing my schoolwork as quickly as I could. There was no waiting for other kids to finish, and no pointless busywork. When I struggled with subjects like math, I could take my time without feeling rushed. However, I didn't see the connection between subjects; it often felt like a check-the-box approach with unrelated pages of classwork that had to be filled out in a specific way, answering questions precisely as the teacher's manual wanted. There was no room for debate, discussion, creativity, or connection. Still, I loved the quiet environment of our home; it allowed me to focus. As an animal lover, homeschooling gave me ample time to play with my various pets. Over the years, I gathered an assortment of animals ranging from rats to cats, rabbits, guinea pigs, dogs, wild birds (which I rehabilitated after our cats caught them), and even, at one point, a flock of ducks abandoned by their mother. My parents drew the line at the ducks, and we had to take them to a rehabilitation center the next day. I was crushed and definitely didn't understand why we couldn't raise them in our small city house. My passionate love for animals led my dad to think I'd become a PETA advocate . . . but thankfully, that didn't happen. I've mellowed out; I'm not an animal rights extremist now, but we do have five cats, two dogs, and five rats currently, so I'm also not sure I fit quite into the normal box either.

The Gift that Changed My Life

My parents were gifted a concert grand Steinway piano when I was only a few years old. They felt a deep responsibility because of this gift to prioritize a solid musical education for me and my sister. Therefore, at five years old, I started piano lessons with the best music teacher in town. She was an elderly woman from Russia, and she fulfilled all your preconceived notions of what an old Russian teacher would be like. She was unfailingly strict and highly demanding. I had to practice for thirty minutes every day, and my mom was expected to sit in on my lessons for the first few years in order to take notes so that she knew what we were to practice during the week. I felt nervous before every lesson. I wanted to do well. Practicing wasn't fun in those early days either. I hated having to do something every single day for a set period of time.

Homeschooling gave me the time to practice music, and as a result, I became quite proficient at the piano. I participated in numerous public performances at various venues, from nursing homes to recital halls. I competed in and won Bach competitions and took part in an event called the "Guild," where I prepared pieces to perform for judges who evaluated my performances based on different rubrics. I excelled at all of this, although it made me feel extremely uncomfortable and nervous. I loved music solely for its own sake. I did not enjoy the self-discipline required for daily practice, and I certainly did not enjoy performing. I just loved how music made people *feel*. As I gradually improved and could create more beautiful and complex music, I developed a deep and passionate love for the art. Later on, I added the violin and singing to my repertoire. It took some time, but I finally recognized, even as a child, how enjoyable and rewarding it was to work incredibly hard at something and become very skilled at it.

Why am I sharing all this? Because it's important to start by addressing a widespread, modern misconception that underlies many parenting decisions today. It's the belief that, above all, we must not "make" a child learn anything while they are very young. The idea is that requiring our children to do anything is a form of evil. Somehow, we have become a society that looks to children and asks them what they want to learn and if they want to learn it, rather than being a society where parents teach their children valuable skills and knowledge, recognizing that one day the child will appreciate it but understanding that, right now, they may not—precisely because they are children. Children cannot view their future in the same holistic way as adults can. By their nature, children do not know what is best for them, and that's why God has given them parents. People used to parent in this manner, and they still do in many countries. But in our country, we tend to defer every decision to the child.

We'll explore this more later, but it is a blessing for your child when you teach them how to persevere through difficult tasks and acquire skills over time. It is a gift to instill in them the values of self-discipline and hard work. Although it is a less common approach these days, the benefits are lifelong. Now, if you are cruel or hurtful to a child during the learning process, that is an entirely different matter. Yet, for some reason, people often equate cruelty with high standards. High standards do not equal cruelty. Those two things are entirely separate from one another. You can be cruel and hurtful even with low standards, and you can be cruel and hurtful without standards altogether. Cruelty is a systemic problem within a person's soul; in other words, it is a vice. Vices form part of a person's character. By neglecting to teach your child self-control and self-discipline, you are not preventing them from becoming a cruel person. In fact, you are opening the door for your child to tread the path of cruelty because beneath cruelty lies a total lack of self-control and a profound level of selfishness. Cruelty thrives on these two traits like a fungus. It represents one of the basest inclinations of the sinful human heart, and a cruel person has surrendered themselves to it wholeheartedly.

Leaving Home

After eighth grade, I attended a private Catholic school nearby. The education was not remarkable, though I'm sure it was much more expensive. It followed a similar format to public schools, with each class being isolated from the others. You learned various random topics and snippets of history. I took a foreign language (French), but since I hadn't engaged with a foreign language in my earlier years, I found it extremely difficult and overwhelming. School felt dull and stressful. Then one day during my sophomore year, I received an invitation to visit a pastor and his family who had previously lived in Santa Barbara but had since moved to North Carolina. While in Santa Barbara, I had grown close to their two young daughters and had babysat them many times. I missed them, and so I jumped at the chance to visit.

While I was staying at their house, they took me to visit a local all-girls boarding school in Raleigh, North Carolina. It was a splendid, Southern-style boarding school and very much impressed my young mind with its tall, thick white pillars, wooden flooring, painted pictures in old frames, and dorm rooms. The school offered performance opportunities and boasted an impressive academic program along with a variety of electives. I was won over. It felt like an opportunity to live on my own and have a great adventure. I asked my parents if I could attend the school. I made as strong a case as I could, and surprisingly, they agreed to send me.

The school's curriculum turned out to be nothing special compared to what I had experienced before, even though they charged significantly more for the pleasure. The subjects were, unbeknownst to me, aligned with the same ideological lines as those in public schools. It was a "Christian" school, so we attended chapel occasionally, but it wasn't different in other fundamental ways. Subjects were taught in a piecemeal fashion, reading was not emphasized, and learning remained as dull as ever.

Darkness Takes Over

Those last two years of high school were a dark time for me—the darkest in my entire life. I stopped going to church, and without my parents' supervision, my heart wandered from the Lord. I was too young to be without their guidance, discipline, and protection. As Proverbs 29:15 says, "The rod and reproof give wisdom, but a child left to himself brings shame on his mother." I lived out these words. Although I was very popular, I became deeply depressed and internally lonely. I felt lost and hopeless, and I lacked excitement for anything I was studying because it was merely about checking boxes and regurgitating what the textbook told me to say. School was just a necessary evil to endure until I could get to the enjoyable parts of the day: free time. I don't recall a single thing I learned academically, but I do remember some lifelong lessons I gained from the experience itself. As Scripture says, "God works all things for good for those who have been called according to His purpose" (Rom 8:28). The experience itself wasn't good, but God used it for good later on.

It taught me something very important. It showed me how worthless it is to sell your soul for the approval of others. Popularity is inherently appealing. We want people to like us. We want friends. I followed society's call to prioritize friendship as the highest good, and in doing so, I betrayed my

Lord and myself for two years, and I was no happier for it. I was well-liked, and I made everyone feel good about themselves, yet I felt completely alone and lost. I said the right words and conformed all my ways to the crowd so that I was approved by man, but I did not have God's approval. I did what I wanted (within only very general boundaries), and it made me feel terrible. During this period, I cut my hair extremely short and dyed it in all sorts of colors, wore choker necklaces, and goth clothing. I liked short skirts and fishnet stockings—the whole nine yards. Thankfully, I never did drugs. I wanted a tattoo and even visited a tattoo shop to inquire about getting one, but my fear of my mom's reaction if she ever found out, along with the risk of getting a disease from a needle, prevented me.

I listened to all the rock music I wanted to, which was very depressing stuff at the time, and I knew even then, consciously, that it was making me more depressed. But I was a kid. So I kept doing destructive things. I wanted to be rebellious, and there was really no one to stop me or to hem me in. I learned firsthand, in such an up-close and personal way, the need for parents in their children's lives. Children need parents to be physically present to guide them. This has only strengthened my resolve to be physically present in my children's lives during their childhood. It's all too easy to watch what other families do and think that, because it is "normal" to hand your children over to others, this will also be good for them. Many families consistently turn their children over to educational systems or daycare programs. But reality proves that this is unwise. Children instinctively seek guidance and support, which is part of their nature. If those things are not coming from their parents, they will come from their peers or other adults in their lives, and every one of these influences helps to mold and shape a child into the adult they will become. God did not give other people the responsibility of raising these children, however. He assigned that responsibility to the parents. It is our job as parents to nurture and guard our children during their most impressionable stages so that they will develop into strong, grounded, assured young adults who are emotionally and spiritually prepared for the world around them.

I continued performing as much as possible in high school and eventually received a merit-based scholarship to the Benjamin T. Rome School of Music at The Catholic University of America (CUA) in Washington, DC, a private university situated on a beautiful campus in northeast DC. The courses offered there were intense. I took philosophy, psychology, music, English, French, religion, and many other subjects. During that time, my eyes were opened to what an education could and should be like. So much was demanded of me, and the professors' expectations were incredibly high. The amount of knowledge imparted in every class floored me. There were no videos, iPads, hands-on activities, or in-class collaboration. Just an enthusiastic, knowledgeable professor standing up in front of a classroom, sharing wisdom with the students. It was intoxicating. Subjects I never would have thought interesting suddenly became fascinating. I remember hearing that I had to take music history and a philosophy course and thinking how dull that sounded. But the teachers, filled to the brim with information and passionate about their subjects, quickly won me over. I remember feeling giddy coming out of my classes, often calling my dad during the day just to share all the incredible things I had learned.

God's Calling & Finding Our Path

During that time, I also started attending church again. This occurred through a series of unusual events, but it's enough to say that God was clearly calling me back. It was my freshman year of college; I had just turned eighteen, and on a cold Sunday in January, I met a Marine at the church. We dated throughout my college years. During that period, he left the Marine Corps and enrolled at Indiana University in Bloomington, Indiana. We continued our relationship, and on the day he graduated from college, December 19, 2009, we were married. At that point, I was a middle school teacher in Virginia, and my husband, Richard, became a freelance trombone player, performing with symphonies and big bands in the area. He also managed a music studio. We lived a very simple life together. A few years later, I became pregnant with our first child, and we were elated.

We reached a crossroads then and there. Would I continue teaching after the baby was born, or would I leave teaching to care for my child at home? We didn't have the money for me to stop teaching; we relied heavily on the income I was bringing in. We had to discuss our options because raising our child ourselves was our top priority.

Richard decided to join the Army to support the family around the time our daughter, Irene, was born. Soon afterward, we moved. Having my daughter and being at home with her all day long gave me plenty of time to observe how she learned. She was always so interested in books and information. She retained everything—I couldn't believe it. I had not realized how smart children were before then, and it was eye-opening to watch her remember more than I ever expected.

Irene was about two years old when I met a new friend named Trista, who had a son around the same age as my daughter. She showed me how she was teaching her son all sorts of things. Learning posters filled his room, showing how to count to one hundred, the days of the week, the months, colors, and shapes. He knew all the information, and I was amazed! She told me about a reading book that a friend of hers had used to successfully teach all seven of her children to read. I thought I should definitely give the book a try if it worked for all seven children in one family! The book was called *Teach Your Child to Read in 100 Easy Lessons.*[1]

I got the book.

We struggled through it.

Life changed.

There is a bit more to it than that, though. My daughter was two and a half years old when we started and three years old when we finished. Let me tell you, it was a hard road getting through that book. I had no support from friends. Trista, the one who told me about the book, hadn't tried it. I remember another friend telling me how she didn't think it was good to make a child learn something like that when they are young. I had others telling me it would ruin their childhood. I couldn't wrap my head around how it could be harming my daughter to have her sit for 10–15 minutes a day to do some valuable learning. How was fifteen minutes out of the fourteen hours she was awake going to ruin her childhood? That's about 1 percent of her waking hours spent learning to read. It didn't make sense how that is such a huge deal and, in any way, a bad thing. Besides, I was already seeing the fruit of the labor: I could already tell she was learning.

It was clearly evident, yet it was also slow. My patience was tested frequently, as I am not naturally a patient person, and when teaching a child anything, you realize that patience is really quite often required. Children don't immediately grasp difficult new concepts. It takes time. Sometimes I struggled to understand why she didn't seem to retain simple things we had practiced repeatedly. . . . Why do I have to explain this rule again for the hundredth time? I wanted it to click, and I wanted it to click *now*. However, what motivated me was witnessing her progress here and there

---

1. By Siegfried Engelmann, Phillis Haddox, and Elaine Bruner.

at the beginning, and then increasingly as we continued. She did gain ground, and it was noticeable, but it just wasn't a clear progression every single day. It was noticeable progress over an extended period of time. I have since learned much more about what actually happens in the brain when a child learns to read. I now understand why it takes so long for it to "click," but back then, I wasn't sure what was going on.

Once my daughter learned to read, our lives changed. She would walk into the grocery store, and her eyes would light up as she realized she could read what was written all around her. She picked up book after book and entered new worlds all on her own, which sparked a variety of passions and interests. She learned from children's encyclopedias and DK informational books scattered throughout the house. She read everything she could get her hands on, and we made sure to add only high-quality books to our library. She could also entertain herself at doctor's appointments and in the car, which was extremely helpful. The most amazing part was that her reading skills skyrocketed. The trajectory of her reading abilities, which began slow and inconsistent, eventually tore through the roof.

Unbeknownst to me, teaching a child to read at a young age enables reading skills to become second nature for them. This, in turn, allows them to engage directly with the material (unhindered by the words on the page). That direct engagement creates excitement, which naturally propels them enthusiastically forward into more challenging literature. The more challenging literature, in turn, produces higher-level reading skills, allowing them to engage with even more material. This material, in turn, excites them and propels them forward, continuing the cycle.

When my first daughter was little, I hadn't really thought much about homeschooling. I simply immersed myself in the joy of being with her and engaging in life with her by my side. But once she learned to read, I realized I was in trouble. There was no way she could go to school at five or six years old after having known how to read for the last two or three years. She would be bored, which would lead to trouble. So, I started looking into homeschooling and contemplating it more. I reflected on what I observed as a teacher in the public schools, and I began noticing what was happening right before me in the homes of friends and in the culture at large. What were kids actually learning in school? How was it affecting them emotionally and mentally? Over time, I encountered numerous reasons to homeschool—reasons I simply hadn't taken the time to consider. I became convinced that it was objectively better for her academically, spiritually, mentally, and physically to be homeschooled.

Oh Baby! (x8)

Twenty-one months after the birth of our first daughter, we welcomed our next child, another gift from God: Esther. I decided to teach her to read at three, just as I had done with Irene. Teaching Esther to read was a unique challenge because she had a speech impediment and would often stare at the wall instead of looking at the page. Her stubbornness and temper added to my frustrations and were issues I had to address daily. However, with perseverance and God's grace, she, too, learned to read at three years old. Despite the difficulties, she became absolutely obsessed with reading. It became her favorite pastime, and she has read nearly every book in the house, most of them multiple times (and we have eighteen bookshelves). She can recall almost every plot and many seemingly insignificant details. To help her understand what she could read as credit for literature class at home, I made a list of the books we owned and organized them by increasing difficulty. The standard was that the quality had to be high enough to count for school and it must promote what is good and true. I kept track of her pages until, at seven years old, she surpassed 20,000 pages, and then I gave up. I couldn't keep up with her. She consumed books as fire consumes paper.

Another daughter followed about twenty-three months later. Her name is Clara, and she, too, learned to read at age three. By six years old, she was reading and comprehending books like *The Yearling*, an over 400-page piece of classic literature. We had a total of eight children over the years, tragically losing three of them to miscarriages. All five of our living children learned to read at three years old, and it was the most challenging and rewarding thing that I have ever done. It opened up both the Scriptures and an entire world of imagination and information to them.

Once I decided to homeschool, the next thing I needed to do was begin sorting through the available homeschool curricula—a daunting task indeed! I felt directionless and lost. Where should I even start? As I scoured the Internet, I noticed that the content available for preschool-age children was often what I was already doing at home. There was no need to pay for that. As time passed, I halfheartedly tried a few programs, but nothing stood out as unique or worth paying for in the end. It wasn't until I came across a classical education program that I noticed something different. I read their educational philosophy and thought, "Wow! I could have written that!," because it was completely in line with my views on education. I looked through their curriculum and saw page after page of content-rich materials, not busy work. Kids weren't spending much of their time in school doing things they already did outside of it, like coloring or crafts. Their literature section was impressive, to say the least, featuring many classic works that I hadn't seen promoted in any other curriculum. They expected children to read significantly more over the course of a year than I had seen any other program require. As a matter of fact, they expected a lot of their students in general. I examined the content and subjects introduced in the later grades, and it made me excited to see where they were going in that program. There were courses on Western civilization, the art of argument, and a class they called "Omnibus," which combined extensive training in religion, history, and classic literature into one cohesive course. The idea of subjects intertwining in this way was a novel concept for me, and while I did not understand how it was done, I wanted to learn more.

The more I learned, the more hooked I became. One day, I decided to make the commitment. We were going to start with that program even though it was expensive, and I had no idea how we would afford it, especially as we welcomed more children into the family. We weren't particularly well-off, as my husband held a lower enlisted rank in the Army, we relied on a single income, and we also had student debt to pay off. I recognized that a classical education required teaching our children Latin down the road, and I had no idea how I would accomplish that. I wasn't particularly good at languages, and Latin seemed far beyond my capabilities. I didn't grasp much about classical education and had only encountered the term "Trivium" in passing while reading through various programs. All I knew was that this classical program appeared to offer the best possible education for my children, and I was determined to give them the very best. I believed that the future should be left in God's hands. He would find a way for us to afford it. And if He intended for us to learn Latin, He would provide a path for us to do so! Looking back, I can say that He abundantly provided for us in every way. Somehow, we always managed to afford all our materials for school. He even provided us with guidance on how to teach Latin!

Now that I have been pursuing classical education for some years, I have seen firsthand its uniqueness and beauty. It is a type of education that equips children to learn and grow in wisdom and virtue. It is a rigorous form of education that transforms learning from what it has become in modern-day America—boring and compartmentalized—into what education should be: exciting, gripping, and interconnected with other learning. A good education always leaves you wanting more, and that is the outcome of a classical education. As my kids grow older, they are becoming more invested in their learning and are understanding how all knowledge connects. For example, my teen daughter is currently reading a four-volume biography on George Washington in her free time because she has become fascinated by history.[2] Why George Washington? Because before this, she read the dozen volumes of *The Definitive Journals of Lewis and Clark*[3] for school, along with diaries and letters from those on the expedition. This led her to become interested in learning about Thomas Jefferson, who sent Lewis and Clark on their expedition, which in turn sparked her interest in the other Founding Fathers (e.g., George Washington). She has woven her prior historical knowledge into the literature she is currently reading to better understand how historical figures and events relate to one another, ultimately giving her a more cohesive picture of history. As she learns more, her excitement grows; she is spurred on by knowledge. Her education doesn't stop the moment school ends for the day—it continues across a broad spectrum of interests, precisely because she has experienced classical education.

A traditional, classical education is not boring. Not because we are doing crafts and activities, but because the content is so packed with information that it does not give a child the opportunity to become bored. They never stop learning, and that is what drives them forward.

2. Flexner, *George Washington*.
3. Moulton, *Definitive Journals*.

2

The Garden of Their Hearts

Our Role as Parents

YEARS AGO, WHEN I had only three kids at home, I had a revelation. Not a clouds-parting, light-streaming-down-from-heaven, actual-voice-of-God type of revelation, but a definite revelation about what a parent's role actually is. I realized that my work was like that of tending a garden. Parenting is like being a gardener, and my children's hearts were like the garden. God was the one who made the plants grow and produce fruit. I did not make them grow. That was not my job. My job was to be the worker, out there every day, tending the garden. My responsibility was to apply the fertilizer, pull the weeds, water the plants, chase predators away, and spray for bugs. I was to be diligent, consistent, and aware.

I was to water my little plants daily by ensuring that my children heard the Word of God. That was what sustained them. I needed to ensure the small seeds were fertilized by giving my kids consistent love on a daily basis, which helped to nurture them. I ought to spray my plants for bugs, thereby preventing that which seeks to slowly destroy them from laying eggs on the young leaves and taking up residence inside of them. This was done by being mindful of what they see and hear. All of these responsibilities that we have as the gardener of our children's hearts also play a pivotal role in what we choose to prioritize during their early years as we lay the foundational and structural elements of their lives (a topic we will discuss in the following chapters). For now, we will focus on the role of the parent in day-to-day life.

When addressing sinful behaviors in children, I thought of pulling a weed out of the ground. Even seemingly small sinful actions had to be confronted. When a child snapped at their sibling in another room, I knew I had to force myself to get up from wherever I was seated and deal with it. When one child displayed resentment, I was responsible for stopping it in its tracks. Even if I was busy, even if I had other things I desperately wanted to do at that moment, and yes, even if other people were around, it didn't matter. I had a job to do. If there was attitude, selfishness, pride, or other sin, I had to confront it. It was absolutely exhausting, and at times it felt never-ending. But I knew that if I didn't address the sin, if I didn't pull that weed out when I saw it springing from the earth, it would grow bigger and stronger—quickly. That seed of resentment, anger, selfishness, greed, or pride was like an invasive plant that would choke the good plants I was tending. It was part of my job as a gardener to watch for those threats. If I ignored it, the roots of that weed would travel downward, deeper and deeper into the soil, becoming more firmly embedded until it became nearly impossible to remove.

I had witnessed this in many families. The parent would ignore sins committed by their young children—sometimes even joking about them or talking about how they just didn't know what to do about them—right in front of their child. And almost like a cartoon character, you'd watch the child grow in their evil behavior, oftentimes immediately, right in front of the parent. And the thing about pet sin is that it never stays in only one part of the heart. That one sin you notice and which seems trivial enough does not confine itself to just one area of your life, staying cut off from the rest of your being. Sin grows. It *always* infests the rest of you. If a child struggles with anger towards their sibling and it isn't addressed (perhaps because "it's just the way siblings are"), then it grows over time to outright hatred between the two children. One child feels the injustice of the other and resents it, hating both their sibling and their parents for their ineptitude, apparent favoritism, or general inaction, and the offending child grows in their cruelty, deadening their conscience over time. The unaddressed hatred in both children's hearts eventually spills over to other people and other things. Bitterness, resentment, and anger grow, and it isn't until the problem permeates many areas of life or creates a major divide in the family that the parent finally sees it as a problem and wants to address it. But by then, it is too late.

What once appeared to be just a tiny weed has grown into a giant sequoia tree. To tear out the root system would take an act of God.

By addressing sin every time it was evident, I witnessed a change in my children. Not a barely observable shift either, but a massive, life-altering difference that put stark contrast between them and many of their peers, not just in behaviors but in their relationships, their faith, and their joy. The harmony of the family was evident to people around them. They were clearly benefiting in all ways: spiritually, emotionally, and physically. The fruit was there.

God created these little plants to grow, but weeds continue to sprout and will keep appearing in our hearts until we die and are made perfect in Christ, that is for sure. Yet, it makes a huge difference to consistently pull the weeds up through the process of repentance and forgiveness. This way, children become accustomed to the concepts of self-control and self-discipline, making the experience of bringing oneself to a state of repentance feel natural rather than foreign. Sin in this situation is not allowed to grow and destroy everything in sight. In a household with a watchful, faithful gardener, many things are different. Siblings do not resent each other because justice is consistently served, and they know they can rely on that. No one is downtrodden for long by their sin because forgiveness is freely given. Love—sacrificial, difficult, selfless love—is the reason behind what their parents do, and children can see their parents engage in daily battles within themselves in pursuit of their calling. Expectations in the home are clear when there is a good gardener, so no one wonders what is acceptable or how to behave, because the faithful parent has made it their first priority to teach a child the way they should go. Their focus is laser-like on what is most important for the child. God's Word is daily watering their hearts, and that Word is the center and circumference of their lives. Parenting according to God's Word is the right path to take, and doing so will have dramatic effects on absolutely everything else.

I have been struck by fellow mothers telling me how "lucky" I am to have children who are happy and well behaved. Their child, they have often told me, is so much harder than mine. They are sure I have no idea how difficult they can be. Often, this is followed by a description of the child's bad behavior, usually right in front of the child. Their child, they tell me, is so stubborn and strong-willed. I have no idea what they go through on a daily basis. The challenges just never end. It really isn't fair, but they just got that roll of the dice!

"*What?*" I have often thought to myself. "How absurd! Why would they think my kids have been easy and my road has been smooth just because of how my children are now?" I used to take great offense at these comments and noticed a bitter root beginning to grow in my own heart, especially since I had struggled so much to raise my kids in this specific way. I knew I needed God to pull this weed out immediately before it grew any bigger.

I took some time to think about why anyone would fall into this misconception of our actions in our home and how we approached our children. I realized that not only were we on very different parenting paths, but our parenting philosophies were completely different. They assumed we were on the same page when we were in entirely different books, and they couldn't explain the outcomes in that context. The only way to make sense of it was if our kids just happen to be happy and easygoing, while their kids just happen to be stubborn and difficult. Their modern view of parenting lacks the ability to change a child's path in life. If a child is inclined towards laziness, the only response is to ask them not to be that way. If a child tends toward blatant disobedience, there really isn't much to do about it except complain to friends, hire a more frequent babysitter, and drink more wine. If a child has a tendency to argue, the parent can only engage in endless rounds of argument until one of them wins (spoiler alert: the child, who may lose arguments in the early years, will win them in the later ones due to greater stamina!). If a child is mean, the parent tells them they shouldn't be that way, expecting that to be the end of that! It boils down to the fact that in modern parenting, a parent is really at the mercy of their child's natural inclinations and tendencies, with no guidance on how to change course and curb sinful behaviors.

That is why modern parenting often amounts to little actual parenting and much more avoidance to keep things manageable for the parent. What options do they really have? There is no solid, concrete way to address any problems. Therefore, if you have well-behaved, happy, and kind children, it must be because they were born well-behaved, happy, and kind. It couldn't be otherwise. Modern parenting provides no solution for the chaos these parents find themselves in. But the truth is, the other road, the road established on the Word of God, equips parents with all the tools they need, teaching them to carefully and diligently focus on the inner lives of themselves and their children, remaining watchful and aware.

This road has not been smooth. Many days in the past, I have locked myself in my bathroom just to sink to the floor and cry uncontrollably out of frustration because I'd dealt with something a million times, and I was sick of handling each and every issue while managing all five kids. I'd rather not. The temptation is strong, then, to ignore the problems and take an easier path. Just stick the kids in front of any screen to distract them so that I don't have to teach them to obey me, and I don't have to face their sin or the sin rising in my own heart. I see the allure of a quick fix. All I want in those moments is time—time to be alone and not to parent. It is then that what is best for my children wars against what *seems* momentarily best for me. The modern world tells us that putting yourself first at this point is actually best for your kids because it's best for you. That is a lie mixed with a grain of truth. We must care for ourselves without sacrificing our children (or what is best for our children) in any way. There are many ways to do this, but the quickest option in the moment is usually the most appealing one, and sometimes the easiest solution seems like the only one. It is not. We will get into that more later on.

We've had to confront things we'd rather avoid on this path we've been traveling, which has often resulted in my feeling angry and even depressed for losing my temper or feeling irritable. There are days when I have been so tired of the same struggle that I seem to always face *within myself*. Why am I not a better person? Why am I so often faced with my failures? Why am I so selfish? It is not a matter of luck, or how sinful our children are by nature, but rather what we are doing about that sinfulness as parents and how we perceive our responsibility. What is our calling? Who or what are we trying (often failing but always trying again) to follow? The Lord, the world, or man?

This contrast between modern parenting and Christian parenting is best visualized through a metaphor. It is like two houses sitting side by side. Each house has a field behind it, with seeds in the ground. The owner of the one house is out in their field day after day, night after night. They're plowing, planting, watering, pulling weeds, keeping predators away, addressing every bug, and every worm that tries to attack their little plants. And the next-door neighbor also has a field. The neighbor also has seeds planted in the ground, but when they go outside, they ignore the weeds except for the occasional comment or complaint, never finding it worth their effort to kneel down and pull them out. The weeds go untouched. When there is excessive heat, that person is inside. When there is a storm threatening to rip their plants apart, there they are looking out the window and wishing the storm would go away, but doing nothing to protect their plants from it. When bugs threaten the shoots, they avoid touching them, and are sure that in time these pests will go away on their own. The first neighbor, on the other hand, does the opposite and never goes inside. They are blistered from the excessive heat, they are scarred by the hail that has rained down on them, and yet they continue watching carefully for every bug and predator. They have not been the perfect gardener, no, far from it. But they have been struggling at it day in and day out. They have endured all types of attacks from every possible threat to their little plants, and they are completely exhausted. But there they are—you can see them from the neighbor's window—they are still out in that garden, tending to every little issue that arises.

Eventually, these two neighbors get together, and the second neighbor says to the first, "It's *so unfair*! You have such a nice garden with neat little rows, and mine is such a mess! It's covered in weeds and infested with bugs, and I don't know what to do about it! You're *so lucky*! I *wish* I had such a nice garden! It's really not fair!"

And you just stare at them.

Clearly, this isn't by chance. This isn't luck of the draw. There is a straightforward explanation, but it is a challenging one to implement, and it requires a shift in philosophy. The focus turns from the self to the cross, and the philosophy transforms from viewing parenting as a bucket-list, life-goal item you can check off once you have a child, to a sacrificial calling from God Himself with all that it entails. It calls for a change in your efforts and desires, your selfish heart, and your willful spirit.

How do people view the sinful nature in general? How do they perceive their responsibility as parents? Is it solely their duty to feed, clothe, and entertain their child, or do they have a spiritual responsibility that requires daily training and teaching? If they view children as beings who cannot control their own behaviors, then their discipline and guidance will reflect that. If they regard children as an annoyance and hindrance to their career, then their parenting will show that too. If they consider children unmanageable, then that is how they will be treated.

Holding a much higher view of children is important; in fact, it's vital and biblical. Children are a gift from God, the likes of which hold no equal. They are made in the image of God; they are intelligent, capable, and absolutely able to learn. They were actually designed to learn. They can follow the Lord and can control their behaviors with teaching and training. As soon as a child can do a bad or sinful behavior, then they can also learn *not* do that bad or sinful behavior. The idea that children cannot exhibit self-control is preposterous. Think of a dog that wants to eat its owner's burger off the table but sits and waits instead. That is self-control. We see that dogs can exhibit self-control, yet we assume a child cannot be taught the same? They cannot learn, for example, never to take a toy away from another child, never to hit someone, or not to talk back? They cannot learn to be patient, respectful, or obedient? Of course not. That notion is absurd.

As soon as a child is capable of demonstrating their sin, they can and should receive a consequence for that sin and learn not to do it. When our children were able to crawl and would crawl up to a light socket to try to put their fingers in it, I would say "No!" and they'd turn and stare at me. Each kid had to decide whether to obey or disobey what Mommy said. When they tried to disobey, I would immediately get up, smack their hand, and say, "No! Do not touch that!" The little one would cry, and I would comfort them, assuring them of their forgiveness and of how much I love them. We would move on right away, and I would keep a watchful eye on them to ensure they did not try to disobey me again. Even as crawling babies, they learned that when Mommy says "no," it means no. When Mom says "stop," you immediately stop. Many parents struggle to follow through with their children on behavior issues like this, which not only undermines authority as a parent but also teaches a dangerous lesson: when mom or dad says "no," they do not mean it. When you say "no," you must keep your eye on your child and follow through with a consequence if they disobey you. This is the training ground. Your attention to their behavior and your subsequent response to it sets the boundaries for them in the future. Do not say "no" and then turn around and do something else, or say "no" and then, when the child disobeys, start repeating yourself. A consequence—decisive, quick, and clear—is required, and only that will mark the boundaries for future behavior choices.

This has made life much easier, happier, and safer! To give a recent example, I was walking out of a school supply store in town with all five of my children, and we were briskly making our way to the car. My daughter had her head turned sharply to the right, looking at something that had caught her attention, yet she was maintaining her speedy pace to the car. Suddenly, I yelled "Stop!," and she halted dead in her tracks. A cement pillar was not more than one inch from her face. She was about to smack right into it. I praised her for listening and obeying so quickly, explaining how her immediate compliance had helped save her from getting hurt. This is to barely scratch the surface of the real-life implications of teaching your child obedience. There are numerous daily examples that demonstrate how obedience makes life more enjoyable and easier for both you *and* your child.

Remember too that if your child refuses to yield their will to you as their parent, who is standing right in front of them and to whom God has commanded them to obey,[1] then they will certainly not yield their will to God, whom they have not yet seen. We do not want our children to have a hardened heart, so we work to keep it tender and open to correction. This process also reveals our hearts. We come face to face with how selfish, irritable, angry, resentful, and lazy we truly are when we are called upon to parent. We discover that we do not want to engage with another sinful human being. It is frustrating, stressful, and challenging. We tend to avoid our responsibilities, making excuses for our shortcomings and only accommodating our desires that provide immediate pleasure.

How can I navigate this parenting journey? How can I be a "good enough" parent, fulfilling all the expectations God has for me and those I hold for myself? Parents who reach this point of recognizing the monumental task ahead of them, and of feeling the full weight of their calling, often run the risk of falling into despair. They recognize that they simply are not "good enough." When this realization dawns, it can feel like a bucket of cold water has been dumped on your head, revealing the truth that you aren't who you wish you were. You aren't the person you dreamed of becoming, and you probably never will be. You aren't that calm, patient parent who never loses their temper and lives selflessly all the time. What hope is there then? Why even try? God provides us with an answer right there in Holy Scripture. We are told to find comfort in our weakness because in that very weakness, we can see God's strength.[2] We can't recognize His strength when we feel strong and capable. We don't acknowledge God when it seems we have everything under control. But when we come to terms with the fact that we can't be "good enough" and that we can't get everything right—that we are tired and overwhelmed, selfish and impatient—then we are left with no choice but to take refuge in God and ask Him to work through us. After all, our children are God's children; we are merely their earthly guardians for a short time as we live on this earth. He loves them even more than we do, which is hard to comprehend. And He knew you wouldn't be perfect

1. Eph 6:1–3; Exod 20:12.

2. 2 Cor 12:9.

when He chose you to care for His child. He knew your deepest, darkest sins, your insecurities, and your faults. And He chose you anyway.

Our God doesn't work through perfect people; He works through imperfection and sin. He works through the weak of this world. We are weak, we are sinful, and therefore we need His help and forgiveness every single day—all of us, with no exceptions. It is through this very real struggle—a refining by fire that Scripture talks about—that we learn how very much we need God. Not just vaguely need Him, not just appreciate His redemptive work on the cross in some distanced way, but directly and earnestly seek His help in every single moment of our lives. We need His forgiveness when we sin. We need His strength because we don't have the energy within ourselves to do this. We need His guidance because without it, we are lost. We need His comfort because when we fail, we would otherwise despair, and we need the perseverance that only He can provide. We need it all.

C. S. Lewis writes in *Mere Christianity* about the process of recognizing the depth of our own need and sinfulness as believers. He compares this experience to discovering rats infesting your basement. You can ignore an infestation if you make a lot of noise before turning on the lights in the room. In that case, the rats will scurry away and disappear before you can see them. But if you enter the room suddenly and switch the lights on very quickly, you'll be sure to see the rats. In both cases, the rats are present, but only in one will you actually see them.[3]

What Lewis is saying is that you can avoid acknowledging your deep selfishness and how bad you really are if you make the effort to do so. That is possible. You can avoid facing it by organizing your life in order to avoid it. Christian parents are able to accomplish this by sending their kids to school for seven or eight hours a day and putting them in front of tablets, phones, and TVs whenever they find them annoying or difficult outside of that. And this may *seem* like a solution because you are not seeing the side of yourself that you hate . . . and so you feel better about yourself. You believe yourself to be a better parent than you really are because you have created an environment where you do not have to take a hard look at your sinful heart. But in the long run, you are still a mean, selfish, ill-tempered person, and you are not actually a better parent. You have frightened the rats away and into the walls of your house with your noise of distraction and avoidance, but they're still living in your basement. The best way to address them, then, is to face the problem straight on and to see how bad

3. See Lewis, *Mere Christianity*, 192.

it really is. The amazing news is that when you do that, when you face your sinfulness head-on, you will see God's power and strength in your life. He will help you walk this path that He has laid out for you, and it will be so clear that He did it all for you. Taking refuge in the shelter of his wings takes on a whole new meaning then, because you actually need shelter, and you must seek it constantly.[4]

There is a danger in writing a book about the Christian life. If you are not very careful, it can easily start to sound like a theology of picking yourself up by your own bootstraps because we are discussing how to live in the world and what we are called to do and not do. For some Christians, the word "do" in any form is anathema because of its connotations. On the surface, it sounds legalistic, as if we are doing things to get brownie points with God and earn our salvation. Therefore, I want to clarify before we proceed that you *cannot* save yourself or contribute to your own salvation in any way. What I am saying aligns with what the apostles tell us throughout the Epistles when they speak about the life of the Christian believer. We must take sin very seriously, and we should regard following Christ as the fundamental purpose of our lives. In fact, in every single book of the New Testament, we are admonished to watch our lives and doctrine closely. We take this calling earnestly and soberly as parents. The behavior of our children and the choices we make matter because they shape the heart and mind. To believe otherwise would be to separate the body from the soul, reducing people to merely spiritual beings unaffected by the material world.

Keeping our priorities straight is key, and remembering our role is essential. God makes the plant grow, and we tend to the garden—the garden of our child's heart. We should do the work He has assigned to us, *one day at a time*, and leave the rest to God. Don't stay inside your house looking out at your garden and merely wishing it was better. Do not feel powerless to aid your child in their Christian walk. Get on your shoes and go dig up those weeds you see popping up through the dirt. Water those plants with God's Word. Stick it out. Endure to the end. Before you know it, your little field will be yielding a big crop, and you will be praising God for it.

4. Ps 91:4.

3

Setting a Firm Foundation in Early Childhood

Building a House

WHEN IT COMES TO parenting, my dad always encouraged me to "major in the majors," and I have found this to be a truly priceless piece of advice. You simply cannot, by definition, focus on *everything*. When everything is considered important, it leads to the reality that nothing is actually important; either that, or the wrong things become important. Therefore, it is essential that we figure out what to focus on as parents by correctly assessing what has a long-term impact on our children, and then keeping those things front and center in our lives as we raise our kids.

I find it helpful to think of raising children using different analogies. I appreciate being able to visualize things in my head. The garden analogy from the last chapter is one I find valuable when considering my job as a parent holistically. When I reflect on early childhood in particular, I envision building the framework of a simple, small, one-room house, like one of those "tiny homes." First, a solid foundation must be laid, followed by the installation of four main structural elements to support the house. I also need walls to surround everything, which connect to the supporting beams. Finally, of course, I need a roof. With the main framework established, I know that the rest of the building will come together. I'll have a clear idea of where I'm heading and what I should do as I build. The framework, which is so essential, will guide me in the right direction while the construction is underway. Because parents often feel tremendous pressure to do everything for and with their kids, it's easy for the blueprint of the house to become lost or confused. Therefore, we need to clarify our priorities to ensure we complete the structure we set out to build.

What are the basic structural elements of the house we are building in early childhood?

The first and most fundamental element of any house is the foundation. The foundation of this particular house is God's Word. On top of this solid foundation are the four main supporting elements that form the framework of our house: discipline, great books, vetted screens, and active play. Connecting to each of these are the walls of our home, which are formed from unconditional love. Finally, every house needs a roof. Parental protection is the roof of this house. As parents, we are responsible for providing safety and security to our children to the best of our ability.

Let's unpack all of that. We will start with the foundation of the house. The foundation is clearly the most important part of any building. Without a solid foundation, the house won't stay upright for long. It might not even be able to be completed! The lines of the old hymn, "On Christ the solid rock I stand, all other ground is sinking sand," are more than a nice-sounding song. It is true: all other ground really is sinking sand. And who wants to build their house on sand? Not you!

Building your child's early years on the foundation of Christ himself is more important than anything else. It may be tempting to say, "I already do that. I take my kid to church on Sundays." While that is important, it is not what is meant here by setting Christ as the foundation. A foundation is consistently used in a house; it is always found to be tried and true. There isn't a single day, or even a minute, when your foundation isn't actively necessary to keep your house upright. It is essential to all other elements of your home, and the success of every part of it literally rests on this foundation. No matter what beautiful structure you have placed on top of your foundation, if that foundation isn't built on solid ground, it doesn't matter. If the foundation falters or cracks, or if the ground shifts beneath it, your house is in jeopardy. Over time, the structural integrity of your house is compromised, and eventually, it will collapse.

Taking your child to church on Sunday is important. That is part of laying a firm foundation. However, that is only part of it. We want to ensure our child puts their full trust and faith *consciously* in Jesus Christ. How do we teach our child to do that?

Before we discuss how, we should first ask a more fundamental question: Should we teach our children to have faith in Jesus Christ? I have heard some Christian parents say they do not believe we should teach our children about Jesus. There are those who think their child ought to come to faith "on their own." They view their own faith as a choice made at some point in their lives, and therefore, they believe their kids will either come to it by themselves someday or not. "Choice" and "freedom" are used to explain this perspective, while "forcing" is the word assigned to the alternative. If you teach your child the truth about Jesus, you are forcing them to have faith in God.

Leaving the eternal salvation of your child's soul up to chance and the world is both dangerous and almost certainly fatal. In no other area of safety, health, or matters of life and death do we leave it up to our children to simply decide for themselves, and make no mistake, this is indeed a matter of life and death. We don't let our child decide whether they will buckle their seat belt, visit the doctor, or take medicine when they need it. We also would not permit our child to decide if they want to jump off a cliff, walk in front of moving cars, go down a dark alley alone at night, or go home with a stranger. We don't even let them decide if they want to brush their teeth or go to sleep at night! Furthermore, we do not leave any other learning up to chance. We do not tell our child, "If you decide that someday you should learn math, then you can learn math! But for now, I will not teach you math since you need to decide that for yourself." Of course not! It is our responsibility as parents to ensure our children are taught what they need to know for their future, health, and safety. Fundamentally, we understand as parents that we are responsible for ensuring our children know the truth.

Why, then, would we leave a child to decide whether they want to know Jesus Christ or not? He is true—nothing is truer than that He exists and came to earth to die for the sins of the world—and knowledge of Him is essential to eternal life. We can introduce them to Jesus and teach them about the Bible, so why should we deny them that life-altering, impactful, and necessary knowledge? What could possibly be more important than the eternal salvation of your child's soul? St. Paul says he would wish that he were cut off from salvation if it meant that the Jews would be saved, because that is how much he loved that entire race of people.[1] An entire

---

1. St. Paul writes in Rom 9:3, "For I could wish that I myself were cursed and cut off from Christ for the sake of my people."

THE ROAD LESS TRAVELED

race of people, meaning St. Paul did not even know many of them, yet he said he would give up his salvation if it were possible to save them by doing so. If that was St. Paul's attitude towards total strangers, what should our attitude as parents be towards our own flesh and blood? Do we not love our children even more than random people? Should we not adopt at least the same attitude about their salvation that Paul had for strangers, wanting their salvation above our own?

I will use a metaphor to explain this more clearly. Let's say you and your child are on a ship when it hits something and tears the boat apart, leaving you both in the water. You know how to swim. Your child has not yet learned how to swim. Would you focus on yourself, ensuring you reach safety before looking around for your child? Would you simply make sure the life preserver is around your waist, thinking to yourself that your child will figure out how to find a life preserver if they really want it? Of course not! In that moment, you recognize that this is about your child's very life. Nothing is more important than that. It doesn't matter for even a second if your child understands the mortal danger they are in or not. That is completely irrelevant. Any parent worth their salt would fixate on their child's needs in that moment. They would rather drown trying to push their child to the surface and to safety than leave their child in the water to figure it out while they save themselves. Obviously, this analogy falls short in some ways because we cannot save ourselves in terms of salvation. But we can and should put every effort into bringing our children to life-saving faith in Jesus by teaching them the Bible and doing our job as parents to train them daily in the way they should go.[2] Focusing only on our own faith and salvation while leaving our child to figure it out for themselves is incredibly selfish and puts our child in mortal danger.

How do we lead them to Christ, you may ask? We can start by ensuring our child hears the Bible every single day. The Bible is the voice of *their* Shepherd. "But they're too young. They can't understand it!" Says who? Does not the God who made the universe—who wove together every atom to form every complicated cell that makes up every tiny detail of every single living thing around you—also have the ability to communicate even to little children? Cannot He who can communicate to the stars and seas, sun, and rain communicate also to a small child? Did not God say, "Let the little children come to me and do not hinder them, for theirs is the kingdom of heaven?"[3]

2. Prov 22:6.
3. Matt 19:14.

Many parents incorporate Bible stories into their children's day, which is fine, but a special promise is given to your child when they hear the actual words of God Himself. St. Paul writes in Rom 10:17, "Faith comes from hearing, and hearing *by the Word of God*" (emphasis added). Faith comes from hearing the Word of God, not from hearing Bible stories. Bible stories are not God's direct words, and there is no promise attached to them. While they can have a place in our children's lives, they cannot replace Scripture itself. It is essential to remember this as we seek to strengthen and grow our children's faith. Your child needs to hear the Bible for themselves, directly, straight from Jesus' lips to their own ears, so to speak, starting from infancy or as soon as you read this.

Some may object, saying, "They hear the Word in church on Sunday, so that is plenty!" But just as you wouldn't give your child a drink of water only on Sundays or food only on Sundays, they shouldn't receive nourishment for their souls solely on Sundays. The Bible is nourishment for their soul. Remember how Jesus told the devil during his temptation, "It is written, man shall not live by bread alone, but by every word that comes from the mouth of God."[4] That is true. The Bible is food for your soul and for their young souls as well.

Since hearing the Word of God is essential to faith, I have found it helpful to include this important task in our "morning chore" list to ensure we read the Bible every day. I have noticed that if it is not assigned a specific time and incorporated into that time as a habit, it simply doesn't happen. In our family, "morning chores" are just a list of tasks the kids need to complete before school starts every morning. The chore lists include things like:

Make your bed

Brush your teeth

Brush your hair

Feed the cats

Water the plants

Read the Bible

Pick up your room

Practice your Bible memory verse(s)

4. Matt 4:4.

I have to set aside a special time for the Bible in my day, too; otherwise, I won't read it. I make it a point to get up every day (very early!) before the kids wake up to read the Bible. I know that even with the best of intentions, if I don't read it before everyone is up, then the day will go by without my hearing the life-giving words of my Heavenly Father, spoken directly to me. I also love the impact it has on my day. Starting the day with God's Word puts everything else on the right track.

I want my kids to hear the life-giving words of their Shepherd every day, too. When they were too young to read the Bible for themselves, they would listen to me or one of their sisters read it aloud. This ensured that every child heard the Bible, one way or another.

Memorizing Scripture is also part of the morning chore list. When our children were very young, they would memorize only a verse or two, but now they focus on memorizing entire chapters. Even when our youngest was four years old, she managed to memorize very short psalms. They will benefit from this for the rest of their lives. I did not memorize Scripture on my own until I got to college. I remember sitting on a tour bus during the summer of my freshman year while on a choral tour in Eastern Europe with my Bible open in my lap. I had flipped to 1 Cor 13:4–8, which is the "love is patient, love is kind" set of verses, and I decided I should memorize them. Learning those verses turned out to be more impactful than I had initially realized was possible.

Since then, these verses have periodically come to mind and continue to aid me at various times, even after all these years. As the Scripture says, "For our struggle is not against flesh and blood, but against the rulers, against the authorities, against the powers of this dark world and against the spiritual forces of evil in the heavenly realms."[5] This means that our battle as Christians in this life are against the spiritual forces of evil. This is the battle for all Christians of every age and in every generation, and our children face the same spiritual battles. They are little warriors in the faith.

How can we and our children combat such powerful forces? The Bible answers that for us, too: "Take the helmet of salvation and the sword of the Spirit, which is the word of God."[6] By having our children memorize the Bible, we equip them with a sword to wield in their own spiritual battles. We ensure they are prepared for the conflict they entered into the day they were baptized and marked as one redeemed. What warrior enters battle without

5. Eph 6:12.
6. Eph 6:17.

a weapon? That would spell certain death for anyone. A weapon is essential, and our children's knowledge of the Bible is equally vital. It is not optional, replaceable, or better left until a later time. You wouldn't think it best to hand someone a weapon after they have faced years of battle, enduring pain and injury. If you had the choice and wanted them to succeed in their fight, you would arm them right away, at the very beginning of the conflict. It is now that your child needs their sword. It is this very moment that your child must know the Word of God. Not tomorrow. Not later. Now.

What else can we do to encourage our children to desire a relationship with Jesus Christ? Prayer at mealtime is important and part of the Christian life, but a twice-a-day "thank you," no matter how genuine, does not capture what is meant here by having a relationship. There are so many ways and various types of conversations that can happen daily between us and our children that involve the Lord. We do not need to force these exchanges either, because God provides many natural and organic ways to connect back to Him. When you, as the parent, are mindful of this, you will discover that these opportunities are ever present, just like He is.

Even a fire engine's siren can connect us back to God. When we hear a siren in our family, we know someone is hurt or suffering in some way. They may be scared or dying, so we say, "God have mercy, somebody is hurt." The children understand that we should pray for them. This small acknowledgment takes a child (and the adult) outside of themselves for a moment. It shifts our inward focus and encourages us to think about someone else for a few seconds. The kids automatically pray now when we hear a siren. Just the other day, we were doing something, and my toddler said, "God have mercy, somebody is hurt." I hadn't heard the siren off in the distance, but she had. We stopped and prayed.

Or let's say you receive notice during the day that someone you know is struggling and in need of prayer. You can stop, gather your children, and pray for that person together as a family instead of stopping to pray in your head. When you are having a good day or experience God's help in some way, you can express it verbally, giving thanks to God for His mercy and blessings, instead of quickly thanking Him silently. On those days when you struggle with energy, patience, or fear, telling your children about it and praying with them for God's help truly makes a world of difference for both you and them. They get to learn how to handle those feelings because they will encounter them sooner rather than later, and you know that "whenever two or three are gathered in my name, there am I with them."[7]

Addressing the relationship problems our children face and discussing how we should respond to these issues is a natural way to connect daily life back to God. In these moments, children learn how to respond, by emphasizing mercy and forgiveness, as well as prayer for others, and in this way, we teach them to view their future problems through a Christian lens rather than leaving them to react according to their sinful nature. As parents, we can utilize any natural, organic means to continually connect back to our foundation, which is Jesus Christ. It will then become instinctual for our children to do the same. They will begin to relate things back to the Lord on their own and within their own experiences. It truly comes down to simply noticing what God is doing in our lives and our need for Him that will make a difference in this area.

What about desires and dreams? How do we approach these types of conversations? The Disney version of the American dream tells children that they can and should be whatever they want to be when they grow up. It is their right to achieve it. Their desires are good because they are their own, and nothing should stand in their way. Parents can inadvertently encourage an inflexible attitude in their children, which can lead to a sense of entitlement. Any change in course, therefore, will be met with irritability, despondency, or anger.

We can and should have hopes and dreams, goals and wishes as Christians, but we are supposed to mean it when we say "thy will be done," as we do in the Lord's Prayer. This flexible attitude, this willingness to let God be God and recognize that we are not God and therefore cannot know what is best for us—that attitude is best fostered in early childhood.

When it comes to desires, I think it is helpful to remind our children to include in their petitions, "If it is your will." We should bring every care and concern to our Lord, it is true, but sometimes what we want is not what God wants for us. We don't truly know what is best for us, not really. We can trust that if we receive a "no" regarding our desire, it is because God has something better planned for us. We may one day understand why it was better for us that He said "no" to that particular thing we wanted so badly, but we may also never have a clue! We can trust one thing, though: that He is a good and faithful God who "does not delight to bring sorrow or grief

---

7. Matt 18:20.

to the children of men."⁸ He is a merciful father who enjoys giving us good gifts.⁹ He wants what is best for us, and He is working all things for our good.¹⁰ So we ask God for all the things we desire and need, and we bring to Him our fears and concerns about even the tiniest things, knowing that He loves us more than anything else in all creation.

This way of discussing things seeps into conversations about our children's education. We know God made us to delight in learning and grow in wisdom. We should value our education because God has gifted it to us, and we want to equip ourselves for every good work in the future. We want to be ready to do whatever God has planned for us. How should we then approach our work? We should "work as for the Lord and not for man."¹¹ We desire to do our chores and schoolwork with a good attitude, not resentfully, building a habit of how to approach all the work that God gives us, no matter how small or menial the task may seem. This is how they learn to think in a new way about their lives.

While we want our children to have dreams, hopes, and wishes, we also want to encourage them to remember that God already has an incredible plan for them, and they can always trust in that plan. If we help our children establish a relationship with God that is built on complete trust and a willingness to let God be God, they will lead a more peaceful life and have greater assurance in their future. They can rest securely and not be overwhelmed if things take a different direction, which they almost certainly will. What God has planned and prepared for them is, by definition, what will be best for them. They can look forward to discovering what that plan is.

There is no end to the moments God provides where a parent has the opportunity to impact and train a child in His way. We just need to be aware of them! In Proverbs, we are given a precious promise. We are told, "Train up a child in the way he should go; even when he is old, he will not depart from it."¹² We can cling to that promise. If we train them up in His way, they will not depart from it when they are old. Period. No exceptions. We are

8. Lam 3:33.

9. "If you, then, though you are evil, know how to give good gifts to your children, how much more will your Father in heaven give good gifts to those who ask him!" Matt 7:11.

10. Rom 8:28.

11. Col 3:23.

12. Prov 22:6.

guaranteed that even if they do stray at some point, they will return if we train them up in the way they should go while they are still children. What could be a more comforting promise for a parent than that?

As we journey through life with our children, we discover that the most valuable opportunities are those that enable us to reconnect with God's Word and what He has communicated through it. It is there that the true, life-giving waters flow into your child's heart and mind, and through this nourishment, they will thrive as they were meant to do.

$$4$$

Pillar One of the House

Discipline

WE HAVE NOW LAID the foundation for the house, with God's Word firmly in place at the bottom of all things. What about the four structural beams of our house? These pillars consist of discipline and forgiveness, great books, vetted screen time, and active play.

Let's move to the first structural beam: discipline and forgiveness. "Discipline" . . . that's a word that puts everyone in an uncomfortable place, doesn't it? "Discipline" in American culture has become a term that is almost synonymous with abuse. Very few Americans today were raised with consistent, godly discipline. As a result, they approach the subject with a complete lack of experience and without having ever witnessed godly discipline in action. Unfortunately, many adults today were instead raised under one of two extremes: either in permissive households or in abusive ones. As a culture, we have grown accustomed to these extremes, which have become the "norms." Older people may recount stories of how their parents used a belt on them, smacked them across the face, or beat them. More commonly, adults share experiences of being raised by absent or neglectful parents who did not practice any consistent discipline at all. Both of these extremes should be avoided at all costs, and Scripture does not support either of them.

What does Scripture say about discipline? "No discipline seems pleasant at the time, but painful. Later on, however, it produces a harvest of righteousness and peace for those who have been trained by it."[1] That is from Hebrews. Discipline is painful. Thus, discipline is not using avoidance, distraction, absence, activities, or screens to circumvent dealing with sin. That is not discipline. Discipline is a specific response to sin, and it is unpleasant for us and our children. We do not enjoy disciplining our children; we do it because we know it is necessary to "produce a harvest of righteousness and peace," as the author of Hebrews explains. The Bible clearly states that discipline is, in general, required for all Christians.

Adults are disciplined by God, while children are disciplined by their parents. In Hebrews, we are told that as adults, we all participate in being disciplined: "If you are left without discipline, in which all have participated, then you are illegitimate children and not sons."[2] We must be disciplined by God because we are sinful and in need of correction. Job writes, "Blessed is the one whom God corrects; so do not despise the discipline of the Almighty."[3] We are called blessed to be disciplined by the Lord. It may not feel like a blessing when we are experiencing it, though, does it? Yet time and time again, we are told that's what it is. King David understood this and wrote, "Blessed is the one you discipline, O LORD."[4]

If discipline is a blessing when God bestows it upon us, why should we view disciplining our children as anything other than a blessing for them and something to be avoided? If you're looking for Biblical guidance on disciplining your children, I recommend starting with Proverbs. In Proverbs, parents are instructed:

> Whoever spares the rod hates his son, but he who loves him is diligent to discipline him.[5]

> Foolishness is bound in the heart of a child; but the rod of correction shall drive it far from him.[6]

1. Heb 12:11.
2. Heb 12:8 .
3. Job 5:17.
4. Ps 94:12.
5. Prov 13:24.
6. Prov 22:15.

Discipline your son, and he will give you rest; he will give delight to your heart.[7]

He dies for lack of discipline, and because of his great folly he is led astray.[8]

Do not withhold discipline from a child; if you punish them with the rod, they will not die. Punish them with the rod and save them from death.[9]

Train up a child in the way he should go; even when he is old, he will not depart from it.[10]

The rod and reproof give wisdom: but a child left to himself brings his mother to shame.[11]

My son, do not reject the discipline of the LORD or loathe His rebuke, for whom the LORD loves those He disciplines, just as a father disciplines the son in whom he delights.[12]

I encourage you to reread those verses repeatedly. Write them on your heart and mind. We know that we cannot pick and choose what we follow in God's Word. Just because the viewpoint on discipline expressed in the Bible does not align with society's perspective on discipline, that does not mean we get to throw it out. We are warned there will be serious consequences for anyone who adds or subtracts *anything* from Scripture. This includes adding or subtracting anything about discipline to fit our cultural norms.

When we think about disciplining our children, we should avoid the notion that some children are "more difficult" or "strong-willed" than others. I subscribed to this popular idea years ago, mainly due to Dr. Dobson's book, *The New Strong-Willed Child*, which promotes the belief that some children are stronger-willed than others. However, after raising five distinctly different children, I now recognize how detrimental this notion is for everyone involved. It is also a challenging position to uphold on scriptural grounds. We are all equally rebellious and strong-willed, but we express our sin and willfulness in various ways. A parent might perceive one child as more strong-willed than another if: (a) they do not spend enough time with

7. Prov 29:17.
8. Prov 5:23.
9. Prov 23:13–14.
10. Prov 22:6.
11. Prov 29:15.
12. Prov 3:11–12.

their children daily; (b) they tend to overlook things that are subtle or not obvious; (c) they did not consistently and correctly address inappropriate behavior in the earlier years with the now-"difficult" child; or (d) their own temperament finds certain sins more aggravating than others.

Perhaps one child may throw a tantrum while another tries to go behind their parents' backs. Or maybe one child is prone to lying while another is tempted to argue incessantly. One child might feel tempted to manipulate their parents, while the other prefers to confront them directly. In a family, you might find one kid struggling with generosity and love, while another has difficulties with control and pride. Spotting issues related to generosity and love can be much harder than noticing those involving control and pride! However, neither child is more in need of discipline than the other, and a watchful parent will recognize both issues at play and address them with equal concern and attention. A child's wellbeing suffers if their sinful inclinations are ignored simply because their sibling's more eye-catching ones are attracting all the attention. Too often, the temptation to label a child stems from inconsistent discipline over the years and a failure to acknowledge another child's less overt struggles.

All children (and all people) are equally sinful, and all hearts are inclined toward evil because "the heart is deceitful above all things, and desperately wicked,"[13] to quote Jeremiah. St. Paul writes, "For all have sinned and fallen short of the glory of God."[14]

Everyone is included in that statement. Therefore, the sooner we dispense with the idea of ranking our children according to their perceived sinfulness, the better. This is especially true because this will inevitably be communicated to our children, and that is a very poisonous thing to communicate to anyone.

We must take what the Bible says about raising children at face value. God is very clear. He says what He means, and He means what He says. This isn't metaphorical; it is not open to how you, I, or anyone else personally feels about it. It's literal, and it is in command form, repeatedly. Just as the resurrection story isn't metaphorical but literal, and just as all of Jesus' direct commands, written in the same manner, were literal, we must be careful to listen to what is being said and not read into it some meaning that better fits our modern American sentimentalities.

13. Jer 17:9.
14. Rom 3:23.

It is easy to focus solely on the outward behaviors of our children. However, we want to care about the heart, not just the actions. "People look at the outward appearance, but the Lord looks at the heart."[15] What does that mean? It means we look for our child's clear intention when they engage in questionable actions. This is not usually a mystery. Young children are often quite obvious in their intentions most of the time, and if it is truly unclear, we can ask.

For example, if a child accidentally trips another child, that is quite a different thing from *trying* to trip a child but not succeeding. It is true that in the first case, a child was hurt, while in the second case, that same child was not harmed in the least. However, our responses to these two situations should be entirely different. In the first instance, we can simply caution the child to be more careful. In the second instance, we should respond *as if the child had succeeded*, since the intention behind their action was to cause harm.

Or perhaps let's imagine a very young child tries, but doesn't succeed, in ripping a toy out of their parent's hand in a fit of anger. What should that parent do? They should respond as if the child succeeded in ripping the toy away, since that was the clear intention. If the child had been strong enough or fast enough, they would have succeeded. Their aim was to be mean and selfish, and that is what the parent should then address. Just because a child is prevented from causing harm due to their size or abilities does not mean that their heart is not guilty of that sin. They were intent on doing damage but they were prevented from doing so for reasons of circumstance. We need to respond to that. That is what matters.

Jesus himself cared not only about the physical action, but also about the heart. He viewed murder as the physical killing of a person, but He also considered hatred to be murder.[16] Jesus viewed sleeping with another man's wife as adultery, but He also considered looking lustfully at a woman as adultery.[17] A child's rebellious heart can manifest in a variety of ways, and we do well to be on the lookout for those ways. Like a boat's captain on the high seas, we stay alert and vigilant, looking out over the waters to warn of incoming hazards that threaten the ship and to help it steer around them to continue on course. If the child runs into a hazard, we repair the

15. 1 Sam 16:7.

16. "Anyone who hates a brother or sister is a murderer." 1 John 3:15.

17. "But I tell you that anyone who looks at a woman lustfully has already committed adultery with her in his heart." Matt 5:28.

ship through the process of discipline and forgiveness, always remaining vigilant for the next hazard that might endanger our ship.

What are the hazards? These refer to anything that damages a child's tender heart and seeks to harden it against God's laws. Hazards manifest in various rebellious behaviors, many of which are dismissed as normal and acceptable simply because a child is engaging in the sinful behavior. There are multiple ways to address this misconception. The first step is to acknowledge that while it is true all sin is commonplace—after all, we live in a sinful world—the regularity of that sin does not make it acceptable. It is normal, for example, for people to be unfaithful to their spouses, but does that make it less sinful? Of course not. It is also common for people to get drunk, but does that make it OK? Again, of course not. The same applies to the sins committed by children. The frequency with which children may commit a particular sin does not make it any less egregious or in need of correction.

Another way we might respond to this is by pointing out the nature of sin. Unchecked sin is not a stagnant thing. Sinful behaviors resemble an invasive organism. Many examples of this occur during childhood. A common example you are no doubt familiar with involves food. Let's say little Suzy and her parents are sitting down for dinner. Suzy's mother proudly places a plate containing broccoli in front of Suzy, a plate she has taken time to prepare. Little Suzy stares at the plate and declares she will not eat the broccoli. It is disgusting and gross. She hates broccoli. There is clear defiance displayed directly to the parent. The child is telling the parent "no," and putting their fists up (metaphorically) into a fighting stance. Whether in words or action, the parent is threatened with one of two punishments if they do not comply: either the child will not eat, or they will throw a fit.

The parent, viewing this as a normal and therefore entirely acceptable childhood behavior, caters to this act of defiance by immediately removing the offending item. The rebellious heart not only goes unchecked, the child is rewarded with the parent's capitulation. The child learns that rebellion grants them power and what they want. This is why rebellion never stops at the broccoli. Soon, they will add various other food items to the list, chosen at random. You must adhere to that list with meticulous precision. You will obey their desires. They no longer like tomatoes—didn't you get the memo at the last meal? And now you offered pasta sauce. Disgusting. Take it back. I refuse to eat it. I also no longer eat peas, and you included peas in that. Gross. Take them out. It is entirely self-evident how unhealthy it is when children follow this path of rebellion through pickiness. Living off mac and cheese and chicken nuggets is a recipe for all sorts of future health problems.

Similarly, unaddressed sin always—always—metastasizes to the point where the consequences can no longer be ignored. By that time, the issue has become so significant and pervasive that addressing it feels overwhelmingly difficult. The weed has grown too strong, and the roots have gotten too deep.

Sin must be addressed. It will not simply go away if left alone, and as parents, we have the responsibility to address our child's sin. Proverbs is very clear about this. We help our child when we notice those intentions and inclinations towards both good and evil and prevent them from continuing to harm themselves with the weeds of unchecked sin, which threaten to choke their hearts and souls. We assist our children by teaching them how to repent of their sinfulness, to ask forgiveness, and ultimately to receive forgiveness.

Part of discipline involves recognizing when our children do *good* things as well. When they display virtue, we should notice and praise them for it. Encouraging our children is just as important as disciplining them, and these two things must go hand in hand. Think of it as two sides of the same coin: one side is discipline, and the other side is encouragement. We should not employ discipline without encouragement. Encouragement naturally arises from being aware of both the good and the bad and discussing them openly. We aim to recognize when our child has controlled their temper, helped someone, acted selflessly, or accomplished something else deserving of praise. We want to speak highly of them to others and refrain from complaining about them within earshot. Children are perceptive and sensitive to criticism. We do not want to dishearten a child by concentrating on their sin. Instead, we want them to understand that we see them through the eyes of love, and when we must discipline them, we do so purely out of the immense love we have for them. We recognize that they are intelligent, capable, loving, and sacrificial. We acknowledge their efforts, no matter how small, and we celebrate them with great joy. We notice when they wrestle with their sinful nature, and we rejoice with them over their victories in the realm of self-control.

Our encouragement is more meaningful because our children know we are aware of their behaviors, just as they are aware of their own. Children know when they are being bad—they can feel it in their heart. As the Lord has said, "I will put my law in their minds and write it on their hearts."[18] And they also know when they are being good and when they have made an effort to battle their sinful nature. When our children realize their parents also notice these actions and intentions, that praise holds significant weight for them. They are commended for walking in the way they should go.

So often, we can miss those pivotal moments if our heads are buried in our phones or if we aren't paying attention to what's happening in our children's daily lives. Children thrive, however, on our attention, and they need to feel as though their behaviors and actions have significance, that they matter, and that they are acknowledged. Just as you notice what they're doing, so does God, and we remind them of that. We can also draw attention to how they feel after following the Lord compared to how they feel after succumbing to evil desires. When we are selfish or unkind, we feel worse, and those around us feel worse. When we do good, we feel better, and everyone around us benefits. There is a ripple effect from both good and bad actions.

One way to think of this type of encouragement is to view it simply as empathy: we understand how hard it has been for our child to achieve what they are accomplishing. We understand that it is difficult to overcome pet temptations, and we want to celebrate with them whenever they succeed! They are little warriors for Christ, and they have fought their battles and won with the help of the Holy Spirit! What joy this brings to the entire family!

We discipline our children as God disciplines us: with love and with great concern for their souls. We do so knowing that we, too, are sinners, which enables us to fully forgive our children when they transgress against us. Forgiveness is a crucial part of the discipline process. Discipline and forgiveness must be interwoven in practice. Discipline should never exist without forgiveness. The purpose of discipline is to curb the sinful nature and lead our children back to God in repentance for their sin. And in so doing, we share with them the forgiveness we receive whenever we stray. God disciplines us and forgives us freely, and we strive to show that same mercy to our children.

Before a consequence such as a spanking is given, we explain to our young children why they are receiving the consequence, and afterward, we offer them a hug and reconciliation. By laying a foundation of

18. Jer 31:33.

discipline and boundaries during their younger years, we establish respect and obedience with our older children. A strong sense of right and wrong has been instilled in their hearts by that point, and a habit of repentance and forgiveness has been firmly established. This doesn't mean that sin doesn't rear its ugly head, because of course it still does! However, the children's hearts are soft and open to correction, and they are accustomed to sincerely repenting and seeking forgiveness.

Our children know how much we love them. They understand that when I discipline them, it's out of love, and I make sure to convey that verbally. As a result, our relationship does not fracture, as many parents fear will happen with consistent discipline; in fact, it becomes noticeably closer. This closeness arises because sin is what ultimately separates us from one another. Sin aims to tear us apart from God, and the devil attempts to use it to destroy us. We don't want to give the devil a foothold, even though he constantly searches for one! Our goal is to be unified as a family—united in love and in service to one another. The only way to achieve this is to care about, notice, and address the sin that creeps in and seeks to tear us apart, and to combine that with free forgiveness to those who wrong us. The outcome is peace in Christ and unity within the household.

5

Pillar Two of the House

Great Books

THE SECOND STRUCTURAL BEAM forming the framework of our house consists of great books. You've heard the phrase, "Children are like sponges." People say this because of the rather startling way that children seem to notice and retain almost anything they encounter. They hear something and remember it, seemingly forever. They see something once and talk about it over and over (and over) again. That movie they watched just one time—well, you get a reenactment of it verbatim for the next six months. The song they listened to on the radio or the comment someone made gets repeated ad nauseam. It never seems to end! I'm at a stage of life where I hear something, and it simply goes in one ear and out the other. But not my kids! Whatever goes into their brains sticks and stays in place (that is, if they want it to). I remember picking up two puppets as a joke in front of my children, and I had them dialogue briefly with each other for just a minute. All five of my children retained every word I said, and they still quote it to this day as a family joke. I, on the other hand, being an adult, promptly forgot what I had said right after saying it. "I said that?" was my response to the uproarious laughter. Their retelling of it seemed to me like the first time I heard it!

Children's memories are remarkable, and their minds are like little trapdoors ready to catch every bit of information that comes their way. God designed them this way because it is in childhood that children have so very much to learn. They must learn how to speak, how to behave, what to believe, how to react, and what is valued. They need to learn about others, about themselves, and about the world at large. Their minds are constantly growing in childhood, both metaphorically and literally.

Synapses are developing in their brains, and myelin sheaths are forming along the axons to create faster connections. White matter pathways are linking the various regions of the brain, all of which occur in direct response to the constant intake of information they receive during their waking hours. Therefore, we want to choose the material that goes into their hearts and minds carefully. Books are a fantastic way to introduce fabulous ideas that spark the imagination and support character development in children. Additionally, books serve as an excellent source of information about the outside world. Another important aspect of reading is that the process itself is beneficial for the developing mind, something we will explore more deeply in a future chapter. For now, it's enough to say that reading helps forge valuable connections in the brain and leads to faster processing times for children. Essentially, reading is like a superfood for your child's brain.

Reading has long been credited with helping people become more empathetic by transporting them into someone else's thought process. This experience is entirely unique to literature. In books, you can truly enter the inner lives of other individuals. You can hear how they think (which differs from how you think) and how they feel. You gain access to their deepest longings and can better understand their struggles, pain, and joy. This nurtures empathy in children, which is sorely needed in our society. Countless examples in the news reveal the cruelty of children, even just within the past year alone.[1] While merely nurturing empathy in children isn't the entire solution to this epidemic, a lack of empathy undoubtedly contributes to the problem. The reality is that American youth have significant amounts of downtime, and the choice for parents often comes down to questionable screen content or literature to occupy that time. Children are setting historic all-time low records for reading outside of school.[2] We know what they are

1. Pace, "Parents Speak Out"; Stone, "Brutal School Assault"; Burge, "Fight at Socorro ISD"; Zouves and Follman, "Indiana 10-Year-Old Dies"; Lee, "14-Year-Old Dies"; Treisman, "Wisconsin Shooting Suspect"; Jones, "California Teen"; McDonald, "Marion Woman Raises Safety Concerns."

2. A Pew Research study shows that children who read outside of school are at their lowest point since they began recording the data in 1984. Schaffer, "Among Many U.S.

doing instead, and we can see how this damages them in numerous ways, particularly regarding their sensitivity and empathy toward others. It is crucial that we encourage our children to return to reading good books.

What is a "good book" for the purposes of our discussion? It is a book that excites a child's imagination, is well written, appropriately challenging, and does not contradict God's Word. It may contain sinful characters, but their sins are not portrayed as good, right, or admirable. Evil is depicted as evil in one way or another. Good is shown as good, even if it doesn't always triumph in every situation. There is no subliminal gender messaging, graphic sexual content, or political ideologies intended to reorient your child's thinking and lead them down dark paths. Many excellent books fit this category, though they can sometimes be difficult to find. Some of our family's favorite authors include C. S. Lewis, J. R. R. Tolkien, Robert Louis Stevenson, Louisa May Alcott, the Brothers Grimm, George MacDonald, and Howard Pyle, to name just a few. We also enjoy some newer stories like *Mrs. Piggle Wiggle*, *The Hardy Boys*, and the *Tumtum and Nutmeg* series. I am very careful to know the content of a book before giving it to my children, and I have grown more skeptical of books published after 1950. While this is a generalization, I have found it to be quite true. You have a better chance of finding a book without objectionable content in older works published prior to that time period. The newer the book, the more often I have encountered questionable themes, attitudes, and behaviors that do not align with what we want to nurture in our children. Additionally, I have noticed that the quality of writing tends to be poorer in newer books. Again, this is a generalization, but it often rings true and serves as a good rule of thumb. Writing in earlier times was generally of a higher caliber across all types of literature and even beyond published books.

The average Joe living in the mid-1800s wrote more beautifully and eloquently than many of our most popular authors today. An excerpt from a simple diary entry written by a private during the Civil War reads as follows:

> Under the dark shade of a towering oak near the Dunker Church lay the lifeless form of a drummer boy, apparently not more than 17 years of age, flaxen hair and eyes of blue and form of delicate mould. As I approached him I stooped down and as I did so I perceived a bloody mark upon his forehead. . . . It showed where the leaden messenger of death had produced the wound that caused

---

Children."

his death. His lips were compressed, his eyes half open, a bright smile played upon his countenance. By his side lay his tenor drum, never to be tapped again.[3]

Compare this level of description and vocabulary to the number-one *New York Times* (and *USA Today, Washington Post,* and *Los Angeles Times*) bestseller in 2024, *The Women* by Kristin Hannah:

> Frankie wiped her eyes and looked sideways. "What?"
>
> "Are you out here grieving the boys we lost or your own piss-poor set of nursing skills?"
>
> "Both."
>
> "That means you've got what it takes, Frank. We all went through it. Nurses back in the world are second-class citizens. And, big surprise—they're mostly women. Men keep us in boxes, make us wear starched virgin white, and tell us that docs are gods. And the worst part is, we believe them."
>
> "Doctors aren't gods here?"
>
> "Of course they are. Just ask them." Ethel pulled a pack of cigarettes out of her pocket, tapped one out, offered it.[4]

In general, all types of writing, including journal writing, were noticeably more descriptive and featured a more extensive vocabulary in times past. Higher-level writing adds depth to the reader's experience while also enhancing one's writing skills and expanding vocabulary. In such cases, children will have quality examples to emulate. Therefore, given the many benefits and value of older books, I recommend that they constitute a major part of your home library. Modern literature does not need to be forsaken, however, as long as it offers true value to your children's lives.

Over time, I decided to compile a list of the hundreds of books we own that comfortably fit under the title of "good books" and that I believe are of high enough quality to be considered for a school-level literature class. We have many more books beyond these that serve merely for enjoyment. I created this list to help me remember which books I want my

---

3. Excerpt written by Pvt. J. D. Hicks, Company K, 125th Pennsylvania Volunteers; National Park Service, "Antietam." Another private, David L. Thompson, wrote, "The truth is, when bullets are whacking against tree trunks and solid shot are cracking skulls like eggshells, the consuming passion in the breast of the average man is to get out of the way."

4. Hannah, *Women,* 51.

children to read. I have asked my kids to go through this list for their literature class, checking off each book as they complete it. They can read them in any order they choose, as long as they understand the book and can discuss it with me after finishing it. By the time they grow up and leave home, I want them to have read all the books on the list. I have included this list at the back of this book. You can use it to begin your own home library if you wish. The books are arranged in order of difficulty, based on my estimation from experience and trial and error, ranging from first readers to much more advanced literature.

A "Great Book" is similar to a "good book," but it has stood the test of time and is usually considered to be one of the more influential works in Western civilization. That is why there is such a thing as a "Great Books curriculum." These books have changed how people think over many generations while offering both unique perspectives and distinctive writing styles. They include some of the authors mentioned above, as well as works such as St. Augustine's *Confessions*, Plato's *Republic*, Shakespeare's *Macbeth*, Homer's *The Iliad* and *The Odyssey*, and Dante's *Divine Comedy*. These books are typically included in a traditional classical education, which we will discuss more soon. They are part of my book list in the back because they are books all children should read at some point.

Consider the difference between types of books as you would the difference between foods. Imagine that over the course of three nights, you had three different kinds of meals. On the first night, you indulged in fast food. It was greasy and unhealthy, leaving you feeling extremely bloated. While it was delicious at the moment, the long-term impact was, by all accounts, negative. The next night, you enjoyed a good home-cooked meal. Your spouse prepared a healthy dinner of fresh vegetables and a chicken breast. It was similar to meals you've had before and will have again in the future. You liked it, it was good for you, and then you finished it and moved on with your life. A few days later, and you've nearly forgotten what you ate that night. On the third evening, you and your spouse visit an elegant five-star restaurant. The ambiance is unlike anything you've ever seen before. An ornate ceiling looms above you, with Renaissance-style paintings depicting images of the heavenly realm, and sparkling crystal chandeliers dangle down, reflecting the soft candlelight off perfectly white tablecloths. Romantic music plays softly in the background as servers attend to your every need. The food is prepared in ways you never thought possible, arriving at your table presented like a work of art. Each dish has been transformed into an experience that is completely new and innovative to all your senses.

Time seems to stand still as you savor every morsel, experiencing the whole evening more as a vacation than a meal.

Now, you could argue that in all three cases, you were simply eating food, and that is true. But wouldn't that be an oversimplification of the value of those experiences? The experience at the five-star restaurant was clearly superior in every way and left a deep impression on your mind that will last for years to come. The meal at home was certainly good and did nourish you. It had its value and helped provide energy. It was enjoyable, but not memorable, and that's all right. It wasn't intended to be memorable. Consuming healthy, good meals like that regularly would positively impact your overall health and mental wellbeing. This is how you should eat most of the time, but that does not mean it represents the pinnacle of dining experiences. The fast food dinner was entirely unhealthy, and, one could argue, damaging to your body. Over time, a diet heavy in fast food can lead to being overweight, depressed, and facing a multitude of other health issues. This comparison is very similar to your choices in books, which, instead of nourishing your body, feed your mind. Exceptional books leave a profound impression on your heart and influence your mind for years to come. Good books are just that—they are beneficial to you and should form the core of your daily reading. Then, there are what we classify as bad books. These are books that uphold evil and present it as good in one form or another. It's as simple as that. Whether it disguises itself in the form of the ideology, attitude, language, or family life presented in the book is irrelevant. Such books do not edify you in any way whatsoever, and there is no place for these books in the home. For young children, those books may feature main characters who, for instance, rebel against their parents, and instead of facing consequences for it, they are celebrated. The rebelliousness is portrayed as a virtue rather than a vice, and it is encouraged for imitation. For older children, it might be books presenting radical ideologies or those containing sexually explicit content.

Avoid these. There is no need for them since there are so many other options to choose from, and they only cause harm. There are many good and great books out there—too many to count! The great books are life-altering in ways that are impossible to fully understand until you pick one up and enter its pages for the first time. These remarkable books will change you and shape your character. We want to include them in our home library and ensure our children experience them. We aim to fill our children with good things, and that often starts within the pages of a book.

6

Pillar Three of the House

Vetted Screen time

THE THIRD STRUCTURAL BEAM of the house we are building in childhood consists of vetted screen time *only*. This means we do not hand our children devices or place them in front of screens with broad parameters for the simple reason that we understand that what our children see with their eyes influences their hearts and minds. And that, in turn, shapes them during these most formative years.

Growing up, we had a small television tucked away inside a built-in bookcase in the living room. We would pull it out for family movie night every so often. We could get one free station on that TV because my parents were unwilling to pay for cable. That free station happened to be the news channel, and even that was somewhat blurry. You had to bend the flexible white cord that ran out of the back a certain way to try to get a clearer picture. Sometimes we would visit the video rental store to rent movies as a special treat.

On Saturdays, my dad would sometimes take me to his office, and I would sit in the conference room, where I could watch the old Warner Bros. cartoons like Bugs Bunny and Tweety Bird for about an hour on the large screen they had in there. Since screen time in my family was extremely limited, I learned to spend countless hours using my imagination, and I have many fond memories of doing so at home.

The cul-de-sac where we lived had many children, and our next-door neighbors had a girl my age named Ryane. She ended up becoming my best friend. Their family wasn't Christian, and they had a TV in every single room, which I found shocking. The one in Ryane's room was on almost constantly, and I loved that. I would go over, eager to zone out in front of the TV. We'd watch show after show, and it was never enough. Hours would go by, and I would get headaches from staring at the screen for so long, but that didn't stop me. They also had video games, and I became even more addicted to those. I found myself obsessing over playing them when I was at my house. I'd think about them constantly, and when I finally got to play the games, it felt like blessed relief. But it would be over too soon. Hours and hours would not be enough. It was never enough.

As both an imaginative person and an introvert, I had been content to play for hours alone in my room. However, I found myself less content with using my imagination because I would rather be zoning out at her house. Our friendship eventually grew apart as I entered middle school, and since my family had not altered their screen usage, I was able to read-just. I once again lived a life where I interacted with my environment and used my imagination. I spent a lot of time Rollerblading, climbing trees, biking, swimming, and reading.

Fast forward to my adult years. I only had a computer when I graduated from college and used it to watch DVDs, but I never got a TV. I never wanted one or even thought about it. I watched so many people waste their lives in front of it, becoming obsessed with sports or shows to the point that it consumed their lives. I remembered those wasted childhood days and did not want that for my adulthood. Once I got married and had children, I became much more aware of the issues with screen content as well. I noticed how sexualized and crass things were on TV when in public or at friends' houses. I observed the various types of messaging in shows and ads. A problem I frequently encountered was that TV was a central part of many people's lives, and therefore it was also central to their young children's lives. The TV would be on during playdates, compelling my children and me to be exposed to whatever flashed onto the screen. It was really distracting to try to hold a conversation with a constant stream of loud, flashy noise coming from the tube. Not surprisingly, this also kept the children from actually playing together during what was supposed to be a playdate! I was too shy and embarrassed to ask people to please turn off their TVs. I found it odd that they didn't think it was rude to leave it on when company was over, but it was such a core part of their family life that they didn't even notice it.

After these playdates, I often went home genuinely upset by what my kids had seen and heard. I felt like a failure as a parent because I hadn't stood up for my children when I knew the content was concerning. I was aware that kids retain what they see, and I knew that once my children had seen something inappropriate, it couldn't be taken back. I felt such a heavy weight on my shoulders between the fear I had of speaking up and the guilt I carried due to my cowardice.

I finally decided I had enough. I wasn't going to live with regret and guilt over this simply because I was too embarrassed and too weak to stand up for my kids. I knew I had to politely ask people to please turn off their TVs when we came over because, in reality, with a TV, you never really know what will come on that screen, whether in the form of the show or the ads.

This was very hard for me to do, especially because it is very countercultural (and therefore I had never seen anyone else do it before), and because I never want to offend anyone or make waves. But I knew I had no choice. I set my mind to it. Despite some awkward moments at first, it became easier and easier over time. Thankfully, people in my inner circle understand now, and I don't ever have to ask. Even our regular dentist knows that we don't use those individual TVs they have in the office when my children are having work done, and it is very positively received and a point of wonderful discussion. Many adults who have passed them in public have remarked on how beautiful and astonishing it is to see children sitting and reading instead of staring bug-eyed at a screen. And it is an undeniably beautiful sight. It doesn't have to be so rare!

We allow screen entertainment in our family, but we carefully monitor both the content and the time spent using it. When choosing a movie or show (one we, as the parents, have previously seen), we ensure there are no ads. I have witnessed the impact of even a small amount of screen time on my children. The younger ones, in particular, quickly become addicted, and I've noticed more behavioral issues when they watch as well. They seem more irritable. When one of my daughters was only six years old, she told me that she often wakes up in the morning thinking about an episode of a cartoon that we let her watch on the computer some time ago. She mentioned that she doesn't like how her brain goes there automatically and does so on a regular basis all this time later. It wasn't the content that bothered her; it was the fact that she kept thinking about it that bothered her. In our family, we occasionally discuss the impact of what we watch, and because of this awareness, she recognizes and reflects on how screen time affects her thoughts. This serves as an essential reminder to parents that children's minds are uniquely designed to process information at a more formative level than adult brains. They are affected more long-term by what they see and hear, and even simple things can resurface for them frequently.

That is why this is such an important topic to discuss, as one of modern parents' greatest temptations is to use screens as babysitters. Parents are exhausted. Kids talk and need things constantly (at least mine do!), so it is simply easier to tell them to go watch something. The problem is that there is a genuine cost to this babysitting, and it isn't financial. It is formative. Recognizing this cost makes us more cautious about how and when we use this form of entertainment.

If you decide to carefully monitor and limit your child's screen time, you may not receive all the world's approval. Society often demands conformity, and the pressure to conform is tremendous. St. Paul writes warning us of society's pressure, saying, "Do not conform to the pattern of this world, but be transformed by the renewing of your mind. Then you will be able to test and approve what God's will is—his good, pleasing, and perfect will."[1] Therefore, we recognize that the pressure exists, but we do not have to succumb to it. We can make independent decisions based on reality and what we know about God's will and His Word, and we can do so without fear or second-guessing ourselves.

The world responds by saying that surely, what kids see on screens isn't *that* big of an issue. You're overreacting. Monitoring their screen time to such an extent would be very Puritan-like of you. And who wants to be accused of *that*? You've seen those shows poking fun at people who object to things because of their conscience or faith, haven't you? Those Christians who are a total laughingstock and the brunt of jokes? Seriously, you really should watch yourself so you don't fall into that category of complete losers!

C. S. Lewis discusses how the accusation of being a Puritan is used against Christians who strive after virtue. In his book *The Screwtape Letters*, which records the fictional correspondence between two demons, the demon Screwtape states that one of their greatest triumphs has been in taking the word "Puritanism" and turning it into a truly repulsive concept—one so hideous that people make a conscious effort to avoid such a label. Screwtape

1. Rom 12:2.

writes that by doing this, "we [the demons] rescue annually thousands of humans from temperance, chastity, and sobriety of life."[2]

The excuses can really start flowing at this point—the point at which one has decided that the worst thing in the world would be the accusation of trying to be too pious. What our kids are watching isn't *really* sinful anyway; it's just normal shows that other kids are watching. Besides, this stuff is just everywhere! You really couldn't avoid it unless you made a huge effort, in which case you'd fall into that Puritan category again, trying to show how self-righteous you are. And you wouldn't want people accusing you of that, would you? No one would want to be your friend if you did that. Besides, kids are not really all *that* impacted by what they see on the screens. It's an exaggeration to say that they are. It goes in one ear and out the other, just like it does with all of us! As long as you go to church on Sunday, the impact will be minimal!

Grace Kelly, an iconic and stunningly beautiful American movie actress of the 1950s, married the Prince of Monaco, Rainier III, giving up her acting career for a new role as queen of Monaco. In a captivating interview in 1982 with Pierre Salinger for ABC's *20/20*, she mentioned knowing a teacher in Monaco who dreaded recess every day because the children acted out what they had seen on television, describing it as "pretty rough and violent." She reflected:

> It's one of the problems of our time. But I always think that because something is possible doesn't mean it is always desirable. . . . We're going through this sort of experience now with television because it's possible it should be on all the time and everyone should be watching everything, and it's become a babysitter. . . . So for children, it can be very dangerous. And then children become brain-soaked by it and numbed. And I read some statistics not too long ago saying an American child, on reaching the age of eighteen, has seen 18,000 murders and 350,000 commercials. Now that's kind of scary, isn't it?[3]

Watching a Hollywood movie star warn about the influence of television on young minds over forty years ago should be sobering. While the statistics were alarming in 1982, today the average young person views over 3,000

2. Lewis, *Screwtape Letters*, 51.

3. Eleanorfan1111, "Last Interview," 04:41–05:50.

ads per day across various media, with younger and younger audiences targeted to establish "brand name preference."[4]

It is estimated that today the average American child witnesses at least 40,000 murders and 200,000 acts of violence.[5] Additionally, many children engage in simulated violence through video games. The Pew Research Center published a report showing that about 97 percent of teens (ages 12–17) play video games, two-thirds of which "tend to contain violent content."[6] Moreover, most teenagers do not play video games within only one genre, thereby exposing children to even more violent and sexually suggestive content.[7] The Entertainment Software Rating Board (ESRB), which rates video games for age and content, found that *over half* of all video games are violent, and more than 90 percent of them are rated for children ten years old and up.[8]

There are no concrete numbers to show how many simulated murders and violent behaviors children engage in while playing video games. There are, however, hundreds of studies demonstrating the effect of media violence on children's brains.[9] A study by the Canadian Pediatric Society has shown that even children as young as six months imitate specific actions they have seen on the screen.[10] To think, then, that parents doubt their six-year-olds will imitate what they see on that same screen! Yet shockingly, although perhaps not surprisingly, nearly two-thirds [62 percent] of parents who allow their children to play video games believe that the games do not impact their children one way or another.[11]

Screens have become an idol. Massive denialism is part of the way this generational idolatry gets passed down, with the average American family relying too heavily on screen time to objectively assess its effects and risks to their own children. The average American child between the ages of 8 and 12 spends about five hours and thirty-three minutes on screens per day, and the average 13- to 18-year-old spends about eight hours and

4. Strasburger, "Children, Adolescents, and Advertising," 1–6.

5. Reissler, "Media Violence," 6.

6. Harvard Health, "Violent Video Games."

7. Pew Research Center, "Teens, Video Games and Civics."

8. Harvard Health, "Violent Video Games."

9. American Academy of Child & Adolescent Psychiatry, "TV Violence and Children."

10. Ponti et al., "Screen Time and Young Children."

11. Pew Research Center, "Teens, Video Games and Civics."

thirty-nine minutes on screens per day.[12] These are not piddly amounts of time but rather massive chunks of a child's life.

Adults often believe they are immune to what they see on screen, which can distort their judgment about the true impact of screen time. The advertising industry, therefore, provides a clear perspective on how viewing influences our mindset and decisions. In the United States, the ad industry's revenue in 2024 exceeded an estimated $425 billion (with 8 out of 10 ads being digital).[13] The amount spent on advertising continues to grow year after year and is projected to reach approximately $592.63 billion by 2030.[14] This means that $425 billion is being spent precisely because of the tremendous impact advertisements have on the population. If an ad can significantly change the mindset of adults enough to justify billions of dollars in investment, it can undoubtedly have a substantial impact on young, impressionable minds. While it's clear that advertisements shape people's decisions and desires, the real question is *how* they exert such influence.

The answer is that ads appeal to people in some way. They appeal to their emotions, sense of identity, or desires for beauty, control, power, or happiness. This is not dissimilar to how other forms of entertainment function. The entire entertainment industry creates content with the express intent of making it as appealing as possible so that people will want to consume it. That's how they generate revenue. When people engage with their material, they are subsequently impacted by it. This is how the entertainment industry has been able to shape American culture for decades. The impact has been so profound that American culture itself has actually become synonymous with pop culture. The ability to transform an entire cultural identity through the entertainment industry testifies to the enormous impact screen usage has on the desires, opinions, and behaviors of millions of people. This is why we must be very careful about what we allow our impressionable children to watch during their formative years. Limiting your child's screen time and allowing vetted videos or shows that you know are free of ads is crucial.

We've mentioned ads as if they are something special to object to, but what are kids actually seeing in them? Let's consider a few commercials aired during Super Bowl 2024—some of the highest-paid slots on TV, broadcast to millions of viewers, including thousands of children. We'll start with an

12. Moyer, "Kids as Young as 8."
13. Statista, "Digital Advertising."
14. Statista, "Revenue in the Advertising Market"

ad for Verizon featuring Beyoncé in a skintight, red, legless bodysuit, which then transitions into an outfit with a plunging open neckline, clearly exposing her cleavage as she leans over a saxophone with the words "let's get saxy" appearing beneath her. Later in the ad, Beyoncé's face is shown on a robot with a tiny waist and enormous metal breasts.

There was also an Alexa commercial with a man cursing someone out on the phone, which then pans to a woman with naked breasts bulging out of her partly opened, short bathrobe as she asks a man "What the hell am I supposed to do?," followed by a naked woman in a bathtub with one hand under the water as she talks dirty to a man in his living room. These things are just considered commonplace and acceptable to air during a sporting event for families.

The list could go on indefinitely, but I don't need to tell you everything out there for children to watch. You've seen it. You know what sin is being portrayed as commonplace, funny, and acceptable *every single day*.

We have discussed screen usage in terms of TV, but what about social media? As you can imagine, social media's influence on children simply adds to the list of what has already been discussed. To begin with, phones and iPads are designed for one user only, granting your child a strange kind of mature access and personal responsibility as they venture into the dark realms of the Internet. Children do not know how to safely navigate such an infinite realm of possibilities, nor can they truly comprehend the kinds of risks they face when using it.

Even with restrictions on their devices, children can access various types of content and people. We experienced this firsthand in our family. I thought we should give my oldest daughter a cheap phone so that when I ran errands, she would have a way to reach me. We used it to text each other around the house as well so I didn't need to shout for her when I was downstairs and she was upstairs in her room. It seemed harmless enough. She was (and still is!) a good, sweet, smart young girl. I had every reason to trust her completely. She knew our rules and she knew the Lord, so what was there to worry about? We gave her the phone. Over a few months, I noticed some behavioral changes—slowly. I couldn't pinpoint what was going on. I would check her phone usage, and everything seemed fine. Then one day, I came into her room unexpectedly and caught her. She wasn't on a pornographic site; she was just on a chess website that she had not asked me about. It seems relatively innocent, right? Wrong. This website allows people to chat while they play, which is a common feature.

I discovered that she had been developing relationships with various random people online. She had no idea who they really were, and I had no clue about what had been said. What had she told them about herself? Did they know where she lived? What if something had happened to her? The more I dug, the more horrified I became.

In just a few short months, several people managed to convince her they were her friends, and to this day, I still don't know for sure what really happened or who they truly were. I explained to my daughter that people are not who they claim to be on the Internet. She could have been chatting with a forty-year-old man while thinking it was a fifteen-year-old girl! I shared information about girls like Alicia Kozakiewicz[15] and how easily people can create a false identity online with stolen pictures, fake names, and so on. In the end, I learned a tough lesson: allowing access to something as fraught with danger as the Internet and exposing my child to the world when they are naïve and impressionable is risky and unwise. All the warnings in the world cannot prepare or protect a child, because children, by their nature, are trusting and impressionable beings. That is why God gave them parents! They simply cannot navigate this world alone, yet that is precisely what they are doing when allowed to explore the realms of the Internet without their parent.

The European Parliament conducted a fascinating study of European countries and the risks children face through social media use. The study stated that "children are routinely exposed to harmful online content on social media platforms such as cyberhate, sexualized content, gory or violent images, content that promotes eating disorders, and disinformation."[16] It listed a variety of widespread effects of the Internet on young people, even admitting that the Internet causes "distorted values and attitudes"[17] in children. They explained that children face sexual exploitation online by adults, as well as extortion and harassment due to their inexperience with adult manipulation. Their warped sense of confidence in navigating these risks independently creates additional danger. The study continues by stating that there is an "increasingly normalized"[18] sexual messaging over the

15. Alicia was abducted and abused by an Internet child predator in 2001 who had formed a relationship with her, pretending to be her friend and a young boy, over the course of almost eight months. The BBC published her story. See Kozakiewicz, "Kidnapped by a Paedophile."

16. O'Niell, "Influence of Social Media," 7.

17. O'Niell, "Influence of Social Media," 7.

18. O'Niell, "Influence of Social Media," 7, 17.

Internet to children, including sending and sharing sexual images, which, among other things, causes trauma. They also discussed various types of self-harming behaviors and suicide ideation content designed to encourage children to think about committing these sins. In this study, they expressly discussed the link between increased mental health issues in children and social media.[19] Obviously, the European Parliament is a secular group with a secular outlook; therefore, the spiritual ramifications of these issues are not discussed here. Yet, I counted at least twenty-eight common, widespread risks listed in the study regarding the Internet's negative effects on children, while they still conclude that the Internet offers "many benefits" to children. This would be outrageous to say in any other context.

Suppose you were going to hire a babysitter and found out that the babysitter had harmed and endangered children in twenty-eight different ways in the past (e.g., sexual assault, abuse, risky behaviors). Would you consider leaving your child in their care? Or if you took your child to a fair and were informed of a list of twenty-eight commonly occurring hazards facing children who take the ride, would you say, "No problem! Just buckle up. It'll be fine. Have fun!"?

Or, what if a doctor told your child to take a medication, and when you ask why, you're informed that every other child is taking the same drug? When you question why those children are taking it, you're told it's to help them feel good. Then you uncover that the drug has twenty-eight severe risk factors associated with its use, including death, impotence, permanent loss of taste, brain cancer, paralysis, and seizures. These risk factors are commonly seen in children taking this drug, and it doesn't help children feel good at all; in fact, it does the opposite. How would you respond? Would you dismiss the evidence and tell your child to take the drug simply because everyone else is doing it?

The point here is that this level of risk would be considered ridiculous and outrageous in any other context. It's only in this one area of social media and screen usage that we find serious dangers and legitimate documented harm to children downplayed to such an extent. The Internet impacts a child's mental, spiritual, and emotional health severely, and so it is at least as important as their physical wellbeing. If we care about things like the food they consume, then we should care just as much about the content they take into their brains. It's that simple. The difference really only lies in how socially acceptable it is to care about the one versus the other.

19. O'Niell, "Influence of Social Media," 7–40.

It isn't just about content or what kids are doing on their screens. For children, it's also about the total time spent in front of a screen. Even with good content that has been carefully selected, we need to limit a child's screen time due to brain development and cognitive issues. Young children exposed to screen time experience "changes in both the structure and function of their brains."[20] The American College of Pediatricians explains that this is because children's brains are highly vulnerable to positive *and* negative influences, and therefore their brains respond to stimuli in observable and startling ways. The result of screen time on young minds includes widespread developmental delays, and as children age, their screen time extensively affects areas of the brain relating to social understanding and communication.

There are many studies available to support this for anyone interested in doing the research, but we will only discuss a few of them here. *JAMA Pediatrics*, a monthly peer-reviewed medical journal published by the American Medical Association, published an article that explains in detail what happens inside the brain when children are exposed to screen-based entertainment. An increase in screen-based media use lowers the microstructural integrity of brain white matter tracts, which support language development and literacy skills in prekindergarten children.[21] What does that mean? It means that the microscopic structure of the brain is impaired and damaged through screen-based entertainment. It affects children on a measurable level regarding their ability to communicate and read. When children are exposed to prolonged screen time, the white matter pathways in their brains are physically changed, which hinders connectivity between brain regions.

Another fascinating study reviewed forty papers and showed a clear link between prolonged screen time and attention problems.[22] Yet another case study on children and adolescents showed an undeniable link between prolonged screen time and a number of alarming symptoms, such as poor sleep, poor stress regulation (due to high sympathetic arousal and cortisol dysregulation), ADHD, impaired vision, depression, suicidal tendencies, and many other serious issues.[23] Hundreds of other similar studies reveal strong connections between severe developmental,

20. American College of Pediatricians, "Media Use and Screen Time."
21. Hutton et al., "Associations Between Screen-Based Media Use."
22. Santos et al., "Association Between Screen Time."
23. Lissak, "Adverse Physiological and Psychological Effects."

behavioral, and psychological problems threatening children exposed to prolonged screen time.

When discussing any aspect of our children's safety and wellbeing, we would be remiss not to address the role parental guilt plays in this context. Societally, we are urged to dismiss parental guilt. Mothers, in particular, spend a great deal of time both expressing guilt and also reassuring other moms that they do not need to feel guilty. The prevailing notion is that guilt is a distorted perception of the need to do something better when improvement is impossible. Consequently, guilt is often regarded as merely a figment of one's imagination. Interestingly, discussions about guilt frequently arise in relation to screen time. Parents, especially those with young children, often express some level of guilt regarding the screen usage allowed in their homes, and taking a moment to reflect on this reveals much.

Let's start by asking ourselves if we feel guilty about objectively good things. For example, do you feel guilty when your kids are playing outside? What about when they're reading a book? Do you feel guilty when you're being selfless? Do you feel guilty when you're doing the right thing? I'm guessing the answer is "no," and I don't either. That's because guilt has a purpose. It serves as an alarm bell that God gives us to notify us when something is wrong. It's like a flare shooting up into the sky to draw attention to a problem on the ground. When we hear an alarm bell or see a flare, we should take some time to figure out *why* we are feeling this way. Far from being baseless, guilt often alerts us to the need to change.

Guilt is a fragile thing. If we ignore it or suppress it often enough, we will eventually destroy it. I believe this is at least in part why parents of young children more frequently express feelings of guilt about their children's screen usage than parents of older children. The guilt has not had time to be stifled into silence, and it is calling parents to pay attention and respond.

Screens are not inherently evil. They can be used for great good. Screens are a fantastic way to stay connected with loved ones who live far away, and computers offer access to an endless array of educational resources for us and our children. Additionally, computers allow classes to be taken online, which can be especially beneficial for larger families with older children. Screens can provide enjoyment. The point here is not to throw the baby out with the bathwater by labeling all screens as evil. Instead, we should recognize the significant impact screens have on children's hearts and minds, and therefore, we should use them wisely and with great caution.

THE ROAD LESS TRAVELED

Content matters. That's the point. What they're viewing makes a tremendous difference. *Unfiltered material* is dangerous for children, and it isn't worth the price you're paying to use it. When Jesus said, "If anyone causes one of these little ones—those who believe in me—to stumble, it would be better for them to have a large millstone hung around their neck and to be drowned in the depths of the sea,"[24] He did not mean simply the act of taking a child's hand literally in your own hand and forcing them physically to sin. Jesus never spoke one-dimensionally like that. In fact, Jesus condemned people for only listening to the top layer of what he was saying and refusing to see the *point*. The point here is clear. Jesus gave us a strict command against causing a child to stumble—a command so serious that he provided a startling visual to ensure it would stick in our minds. Surely, he would include under this command placing our own children in situations where we know there is much temptation they cannot possibly bear for long, and where we are aware that stumbling blocks are ever-present. The worst part of this is that we are putting them into these situations, not out of necessity but simply because of our own selfishness and laziness as parents. We value our free time more than their souls, and we are willing to sacrifice them on the altar of our very precious "me time."

Jesus said, "If your right eye causes you to stumble, gouge it out and throw it away. It is better for you to lose one part of your body than for your whole body to be thrown into hell. And if your right hand causes you to stumble, cut it off and throw it away. It is better for you to lose one part of your body than for your whole body to go into hell."[25] The same could be said of "me time." If your "me time" causes your child to sin, cut it out and throw it away. Find another solution. As parents, we have desires and needs, and while it is true that these needs can and should be addressed, they should not come at the expense of our children. For countless generations, people have taken care of themselves while also raising kids, and they did so without relying on screens as a constant babysitter. It is possible. It just requires a new perspective on our home life. While this approach may seem countercultural today, it is also powerful, and if we commit to it, it can even change the culture.

Life becomes much richer when we engage with our surroundings and live in reality, and this applies to our children as well. However, since this perspective is often deemed radical, we must be prepared for the world's

24. Matt 18:6.
25. Matt 5:29–30.

reaction to it. If you make fundamental changes to your life, they will not go unnoticed. Thankfully, Jesus has warned us about this to prepare us, stating that following Him means the world will reject us. This doesn't imply that everyone will turn away from us, as thankfully that won't be the case, but you shouldn't expect widespread understanding and support if you choose His path. Jesus reminded us of this when he said,

> If the world hates you, keep in mind that it hated me first. If you belonged to the world, it would love you as its own. As it is, you do not belong to the world, but I have chosen you out of the world. That is why the world hates you. Remember what I told you: "A servant is not greater than his master." If they persecuted me, they will also persecute you. If they obeyed my teaching, they would also obey yours. They will treat you this way because of my name, for they do not know the one who sent me.[26]

None of us wants rejection or persecution. We all want acceptance and love. We want to feel like part of the group, and we don't want to be outsiders. Jesus understands all of these desires. He knows our inner longings and created them in us for a good purpose. "How can these things be good if He means them to be unfulfilled?" Ah, but He doesn't! The desire for acceptance, love, and being an "insider" is fulfilled in Him, not in the world. He took the time to verbally prepare us for the world's reactions so that we would not be discouraged. He wants us to remember that we already know how this story plays out and who wins in the end.

The story has played out this way for centuries and will continue to unfold in the same manner until the end of the world. The story goes like this: the world does not understand Christians with our beliefs and our decisions, nor will they accept them. People will mock us, and they will ridicule us using various slurs and slanderous accusations. Christian parents will continue to make countercultural decisions because of Jesus. But in the end, our Lord triumphs, and we will be with Him on the last day because He died for us and saves us all by His grace and undeserved mercy. We will finally be able to live in total acceptance, complete love, and absolute unity with God and with all Christians who have lived throughout all the ages.

The question then is, what do we do? It can feel like a burden too heavy to bear if we're to change our lifestyle to protect our children's hearts and minds. When we think this way, we can turn our eyes to Christ. He picked up the burden of the cross and the weight of our sins and carried them

26. John 15:18–21.

61

for us. He encourages us to pick up our cross and follow Him.[27] When we cry out, He hears us.[28] When we are weak, He is strong.[29] "Cast all your anxiety on Him because He cares for you."[30] A beloved pastor of mine once discussed this verse in a Bible study. He said that the word "cares" in Greek more accurately means to *deeply yearn* for you. Christ deeply yearns for you—to save you, to take your worries and fatigue from you, and to carry your heart's burdens by putting them on Himself. He will carry it all and give you the strength to walk this path. He will lift you up when you fall. He will carry you when you can't even walk beside Him. We don't need to worry about it. We're commanded not to worry about tomorrow but to just take today and follow Him. "Do not worry about tomorrow, for tomorrow will worry about itself. Each day has enough trouble of its own."[31]

Christian brothers and sisters, let us be part of a changing tide. Let us be part of a new era of Christian families who prioritize teaching their beloved children to follow the Lord, caring deeply about what they see and do. Technology can be useful and good in its rightful place, but the content of what our kids see matters greatly. We do not need to look around to see who else is being careful; we do not need to wonder whether or not others may approve. We serve the Lord and not man,[32] and we can declare fearlessly, "As for me and my house, we will serve the Lord."[33]

27. Luke 9:23; Luke 14:27; Matt 16:24–25.

28. Ps 34:17; 18:6; 1 John 5:14; 1 Pet 3:12.

29. 2 Cor 12:9–10.

30. 1 Pet 5:7.

31. Matt 6:34.

32. Col 3:23.

33. Josh 24:15.

7

Pillar Four of the House

Active Play

THE LAST STRUCTURAL BEAM, or pillar, in our house is made up of active play. When you think back to your childhood, do you recall engaging in active play? I do. I have many *vivid* memories from over the years of setting up elaborate scenes for the characters in my room, climbing trees, running through fields, playing in creeks, making mud pies in the backyard, pretending to be detectives with my friends, and creating dance performances on Rollerblades, among others. I also remember creating, designing, and building things. There is something special and magical about childhood, particularly the time spent in active play.

Children have a natural tendency to use their imagination. They possess the remarkable ability to create something from nothing and to perceive things that aren't there. That stick? It's a sword. The pile of rocks? A stronghold to defend. That leftover cardboard box? I'll turn that into my chariot. Imagination is a wonderful gift from God to all children, and it flourishes based on how it is cultivated. Properly cultivated, imagination leads to creativity. Creativity, in turn, ultimately leads to countless other skills and boosts self-confidence. Creativity encourages children to problem-solve, adapt, innovate, design, build, and . . . well . . . create! Children gain so much through creativity and imagination, and often their unique interests and gifts emerge during this process. How can you cultivate imagination? Primarily, through reading! Reading opens up an endless world of concepts and ideas for children.

You've probably seen the flip side of this for yourself: young children who spend a lot of screen time tend to use their imagination to *recreate* what they've seen. They often cast themselves as a Disney princess or their favorite action hero. For many children, this behavior reaches a level of absolute obsession. Their playtime themes frequently mirror the movies or video games they have been watching. Their imagination seems trapped, stifled by such strong visuals that the child genuinely struggles to disengage from these and invent new ways of thinking. There is a noticeable lack of mental freedom, as everything must tie back into what they were watching. It's as if their imagination can only be active within the confines of a small box.

When a young child isn't heavily influenced by screen time, their minds become much more open to natural inspiration from their surroundings, enabling them to learn creativity. Although a child may draw from various books they have read, they are not wed to them as they are after watching something visually. This seems to be because movies and video games offer a passive visual experience, while reading books requires the use of an active imagination.[1] Essentially, the way your brain engages with a screen compared to how it functions when reading a book is so wildly different that the effects on imagination, or even the ability to imagine, also differ greatly.

Books provide children with a general impetus (or basic concepts and ideas) that they can use freely and in various ways.

If children spend much of their free time engaged in active play, they will reap many additional benefits that we can add to the list we have already started. First of all, a child will learn how to manage boredom and, therefore, how to entertain themselves. This is a very important skill for children to develop. Many adults in America simultaneously fear and know little about boredom because there is always some kind of device available to distract them. This is a significant sticking point for Christians. We need to experience periods of quiet because how else will we have a relationship with Jesus Christ? We can't pray when distracted, and we certainly won't self-reflect much or think about His Word if we are always being entertained. Being

---

1. Suggate, "Does It Kill." This is the first experimental work done to test the theory introduced over thirty years ago that "the imager system can be negatively affected by screen-media."

comfortable with silence and more accustomed to taking breaks from our devices is key to nurturing our spiritual life.

Creativity is born from imagination and flourishes when one has the time and space to think in various and new ways about something. That space is often initially referred to as boredom. I have seen my children come up with the greatest ideas for making, building, or creating something after a period of complaining about being bored. I recall one of my kids expressing her boredom and then using duct tape to bind a few pieces of wood together, discovering some large toy cars in the backyard, placing the wood atop the cars, and crafting a wagon, which she then played with for hours. Another child decided to learn how to knit from a book to pass the time because she was bored, and now she knits hats, scarves, and has just finished a 3D Oreo cookie blanket. One of my other kids was unsure of what to do before designing a small portable cardboard playhouse for little characters, complete with handles, which she later gifted to her little sister for enjoyment. There are countless examples of this sort of thing. The point is, instead of feeling we must help our children escape from potential boredom as if it's a contagious disease, we can embrace it as a valuable learning opportunity for them. It won't harm them to be bored; in fact, it will benefit them.

Parents worry about the complaints they will hear if their children get bored. As annoying as it is—and it is *highly* annoying—it can help to think of it as a learning opportunity that ties back to discipline. This is a chance to teach them obedience. If you ask them to stop complaining, they need to obey. This will require following through on your part and consistently proving that you mean what you say, but what will the result be? A more peaceful home where childhood is experienced to its fullest because the children are actively engaged in their environment.

An interesting by-product of engaging in active play is that your child's interests and hobbies begin to emerge. Have you ever noticed that when you ask a child addicted to screens and video games what they're passionate about, they can't respond with anything outside their screen time pursuits? They lack passion or drive for anything besides zoning out. It's as if life has been sucked out of their bodies, turning them into little zombies. This is heartbreaking because children are, *by nature*, passionate and enthusiastic beings. They enjoy a variety of activities and easily get excited when they acquire new skills. They delight in discovering what they gravitate towards—it's a process of self-discovery, and it helps them develop a sense of identity. As a parent, I have learned so much about my children by observing their free-time pursuits. We have seen our kids incline toward engineering, architecture, drawing, music, historical literature, writing, poetry, and sports. Each child has multiple passions and interests, which over time have partially revealed themselves through the time spent engaging actively with their environment.

I have noticed that many popular modern curricula strongly emphasize active play (or "nature-based learning") within their educational framework. Schools like Waldorf and Montessori adopt this philosophy, as do some homeschool programs inspired by Charlotte Mason's work. In my opinion, this approach appeals to parents because they intuitively understand the advantages of children interacting with their environment. However, their children do not spend much time in nature or engaged in active play, instead spending countless hours in front of a screen during their free time. Consequently, their parents seek to incorporate this element into their curriculum. This approach is misguided. When children are allowed to simply be kids, they naturally engage with their surroundings. Parents don't need to prioritize this in their curriculum if they provide what I would define as "normalcy" outside of school. A healthy, normal childhood should involve exploration, reading, and active play. This is very liberating. It enables parents to choose an educational program that focuses on nurturing wisdom and moral virtue in their child while still reaping the benefits of active play.

Active play is not only beneficial for a child's imagination and for learning about their interests and passions, but it also facilitates everyday, real-world learning activities. Children observe you preparing dinner, washing the dishes, folding the laundry, cleaning the house, and performing countless other daily tasks. Each of these activities presents an opportunity for them to learn how to navigate these essential (and seemingly mundane) aspects of life. They not only watch you engage in these tasks, but they should also be allowed to assist. When cutting carrots, you can provide no-cut gloves for your kids and have them cut some too. Just that one activity gives you a chance to teach them numerous little life skills such as always using a cutting board, safely carrying a knife across the kitchen, holding food while cutting to avoid injury, leaning the knife tip down for quieter cutting, cutting off the ends of a carrot and understanding why we do so, determining how much water to put in the pot to steam them, and ensuring the pieces are cut uniformly for even cooking. Each one of these little life lessons is significant to a child and imparts knowledge they can carry with them throughout their lives.

I've had my kids in the kitchen with me since they were toddlers, and while we experienced plenty of tense moments during their learning, the benefits have been ongoing. They now know how to safely bake, cook, and clean up in the kitchen all by themselves. This has been such a tremendous blessing for the entire family and very often a huge help to me. They also understand how to handle all the little daily tasks of running a house, and their contributions help keep the family going. Children are small people, and God created people to feel a sense of fulfillment when they are of help to others and productive. Children are no different. It gives a child a tremendous sense of pride and accomplishment when they can prepare a meal for their family or when they can do meaningful tasks for themselves and others.

It took years of major messes, aggravating mistakes, countless reminders, and more clean-ups than I can count, but it bore so much good fruit over time. It has brought us closer as a family and allowed us to experience things we would not be able to otherwise. For example, one of our favorite family traditions involves all five girls cooking the Thanksgiving feast with me in the kitchen. We look forward all year to the three days we spend together in preparation, whipping up such an assortment of dishes and goodies you'd think we were about to feed an army! We put on Christmas music and have the best time together. They revel in their abilities, and I celebrate them for their assistance. Every skill they have learned makes them that much more equipped to take care of themselves and to be of help to others when they leave the family and go out into the world. That is a great blessing for everyone involved!

8

Building the Walls of Love and Installing the Roof of Protection

Now that we have our foundation and the four structural components in place, we need to surround and connect these with our walls of love. Love is essential and necessary, just as are the walls of a house. Without walls, you might as well not start construction in the first place. There is no point. The structure will be useless and cannot even be called a house. Similarly, without love, your child will gain absolutely nothing from everything you are doing, and all of this is pointless. To love our children well means first understanding what love is, and equally as important, what it is not.

We can only know what it is by looking at God. "God is love,"[1] so our understanding of love must come from Him. Sometimes love is soft and gentle like when Jesus said, "How often I have longed to gather your children together, as a hen gathers her chicks under her wings."[2] But we make a grave error when we think that this and only this is the entirety of love—the soft, gentle, feminine-sounding part. Sometimes acting in that way would be extremely unloving. For example, if your child told you they were going to go mutilate someone, would the loving response be to give them a warm hug, offer them some kind words of encouragement, and

1. 1 John 4:16.
2. Luke 13:34.

send them out the door? Sometimes people need something else for their good. And that is the point. Love is willing the good of the other, as St. Thomas Aquinas said. That is why love is ever-changing and can only be love if it reflects the other in its response.

Sometimes, the good of others is very different from being soft and gentle. Jesus demonstrated this. At times, he called the Pharisees a "brood of vipers"[3] and overturned tables in the temple.[4] Jesus frequently harshly chastised, rebuked, and warned people. Yet if God is love, and Jesus is God, then Jesus is also love; thus, those responses were, by definition, the most loving responses possible for those individuals. The world would not call his words and actions "kind," but that matters little to the Christian. We understand that the world defines things very differently from God and views all behaviors through a distorted lens. Every response Jesus had was the most loving response a person could have, and we can learn a great deal about love by contemplating all that He said and did.

The diversity of His responses to people reveals that love manifests itself according to the needs and heart of the receiver. One could generalize this by saying that at times, people need the law, and at other times, they need the gospel. Jesus embodies an all-encompassing, perfect love, demonstrating in every possible way that He desires the good of the other and finally showing the ultimate conclusion of this by sacrificing His very life on the cross for our sins.

If we want to know more details about love, we must listen to how Paul writes about it. He says, "Love is patient, love is kind. It does not envy, it does not boast, it is not proud. It does not dishonor others, it is not self-seeking, it is not easily angered, it keeps no record of wrongs. Love does not delight in evil but rejoices with the truth. It always protects, always trusts, always hopes, always perseveres. Love never fails."[5] We can meditate on those verses our whole life and gain more every time we reflect on them.

Now, of course, we love our children, and it takes no real effort to *feel* that way toward them; it is instinctual. I have always thought of my children as being my heart walking around outside my body because that is how much I love them. If something hurts them, it hurts me. If something brings them joy, witnessing that brings me even greater pleasure. My children are what is most important to me in this material world. They bring me the

---

3. Matt 3:7; 12:34.

4. Matt 21:12–17; Mark 11:15-23; John 2:15–17.

5. 1 Cor 13:4–8.

greatest happiness, contentment, and fulfillment, second only to my relationship with God and my husband. Most parents would say they feel the same way. I want to sacrifice for my children; I want to be there for them, to listen to them, and understand their hearts, because the fact is that they are not an extension of me, despite how I feel about them. They are their own unique selves. It may *feel* as though they are my heart walking around outside my body, but in reality, they are not mini-mes, nor do I want them to be. It would not be loving to wish for my children to be duplicates of me. Parents who desire this only demonstrate self-love. Instinctual parental love, when left unattended by God's Word, can become misdirected and eventually morph into this very base form of self-love.

We should desire to know our children as distinctive individuals. Even when they are young, they are undeniably unique. Understanding them as complex beings requires our time and attention. People, even little ones, are constantly changing and multifaceted. To truly know someone, you must have consistent contact with them *and* cultivate a relationship where they feel comfortable and loved enough to share their inner thoughts and feelings with you. As parents, it's easy to overlook this second part. We may assume we know our children simply because, after all, they're our children! We can presuppose they will feel comfortable talking to us because, after all, we're their parent! However natural it may be for a child to want to talk to, or confide in, their parent, it should never be taken as a lasting guarantee. It is our responsibility to create an environment where our child *consistently* knows that we genuinely love them *and* that we truly desire to *know who they are.*

How do we do this? Love is spoken and communicated with intention. As parents, we express our love through both our actions *and* our words. When I fail in this, as I inevitably do at times, I must seek forgiveness from God and my children. I have found comfort in the line often attributed to *Anne of Green Gables*, "Tomorrow is always fresh, with no mistakes in it yet." The same applies to the next minute. There are no mistakes or sins in the next minute. The next minute is always fresh. Even when I fail massively and spectacularly, as I often do, I know that the next minute is unblemished and open to me. It is an opportunity to start over, relying on God to help me show my children love in that new moment. Children can be encouraged to view their sins and failings in the same way. We don't have to let the sin of the past moment poison the rest of our day, which is often a strong temptation and exactly what the devil wants. Our failures don't have to dictate who we are in the future, because we are children of God and are freely forgiven by His grace. We are unchained, and every failing we have falls off us like the scales fell off the blind man's eyes.[6]

There are many well-known theories about love. Some theories focus on love languages, while others seek to identify personality types, using labels to help people understand how others think and, consequently, how their personality might respond to certain behaviors. A common thread among them is the idea that everyone has different ways they need to be treated in order to feel loved. Discussing love in terms of different personality types and varying needs has value, depending on the context and relationship dynamics in one's life. These insights can be useful when you notice potential needs your child may have. Does one child need a hug or some time to talk privately? Does another child seem to need a treat or words of affirmation? Keeping your "spidey sense" up, as it were, so that you remain aware of your children's love needs throughout the day is very important. And don't hesitate to ask them, either!

Children share a common need regarding how they experience love: they crave their parents' time and attention in one way or another. This need is universal. If you were to remove time and attention while only providing other types of actions, your child would no longer feel loved. Time serves as a common denominator. Without it, love languages, words of affirmation, gifts, and acts of service lose their significance. There is no child in the world for whom your attention does not convey your love. Think of it this way: if your spouse completely ignored you but gave you a gift, would you still feel loved, even if you typically feel loved through gifts? If they disregarded you and didn't engage in conversation, yet told you that you were wonderful, would you feel loved? What if your husband or wife consistently avoided your presence but cleaned the house for you—would you feel loved?

Children are hardwired to want focus and attention from their parents, just as we desire the focus and attention of those we love. I have found this particularly challenging after a long day of working nonstop with my children, an issue commonly faced by homeschool parents. Before I know it, the entire morning has been spent helping them, listening to them, and providing for all their needs as we tackle schoolwork on top of house chores. By the time we reach about lunchtime, all I want to do is finish school and be left *alone*. This feeling is normal, and there is nothing wrong with separating yourself at

6. Acts 9:18.

times from the chaos, while still keeping an ear out for what is happening. An essential part of a child's growth and discipline process is learning that they cannot always have what they want when they want it, which includes access to mom or dad. So, when a parent requests a little space, the child needs to respect that request and give them that space.

But it's so easy for that *sometimes* to turn into *everyday*, and *as often as possible*. This can be very hurtful to a child, even if you try to provide other alternatives for expressing your love. I've tried it. I am guilty of this. I've tried buying Play-Doh, Polly Pockets, or coming up with activities for the kids, hoping that it would mean they wouldn't need my time and attention. However, no matter how excited they were about those things or activities, they never replaced their desire for my time.

One thing I have found helpful for a larger family is setting aside one day each week (for us, it is every Saturday morning) to take one child out to breakfast for some one-on-one time. We rotate through all the children over the course of five weeks. The kids look forward to their day with tremendous excitement and anticipation. We bring board games to a coffee shop and play while we eat and drink for about two hours. Sometimes, if the weather is nice, we also take a walk. It is a time that both the kids and I treasure, and it has drawn us even closer together.

It can take a conscious effort to carve out that special time for conversation, and it may require sacrifices from the parents. There are numerous ways to achieve this—the options are truly endless—but we must prioritize it. This remains one of my biggest personal challenges, even though my kids are my favorite people in the world! I enjoy solitude and appreciate quiet. Even parents who don't feel this way can find it challenging to satisfy their children's insatiable need for their time and attention.

I've seen the pendulum swing from one extreme of not paying attention to the other extreme of being consumed by a child's demands for attention. I have known several parents who literally cannot have a conversation, either on the phone or in person, if their child is present because their child constantly interrupts and demands their undivided attention. Children who make such demands do so because they know their parents will comply. The parent in these situations always capitulates, and the children only grow more selfish. They have learned to be the center of the universe and they will accept nothing less at all times. We do not want the pendulum to swing between extremes but rather to rest contentedly in the middle. Giving children free and constant access to a parent does not benefit their sinful nature. We are not their personal entertainment system. They need to learn to entertain themselves. However, as their mom or dad, we do need to engage with them in meaningful ways and listen to what is on their hearts and minds throughout the day and whenever it is appropriate.

Engaging in meaningful conversation with my kids daily doesn't mean I have to sit there and do nothing else all the time. If that were the case, we couldn't function as a family because we have too many kids with too much to do, and only so many hours in the day to get things done. Engaging in conversation simply means that I am focused on what they are saying, without trying to concentrate on something else simultaneously. I need to engage with them as I would with a friend or my husband. This may sound obvious, but for many parents, it is one of the hardest things to accomplish, especially in this day and age of technology overload. We have gotten into the habit of being on our screens instead of interacting in real time and space, and so a child's need for our attention often interferes with that rather soothing system we have developed for ourselves.

One way to create special moments is by taking mundane tasks like cutting vegetables or sweeping the floor and using that time to talk with your children instead of listening to your favorite podcast. While you can't scroll Instagram or Facebook and have a meaningful conversation with your kids, you can engage with them during activities like washing the dishes or folding the laundry. Engaged conversation can be taxing (especially for introverts!), but it helps to think of it as nourishing their little hearts with the love they crave so deeply. It really can't be done in any other way. There is no shortcut to this. As we keep that in mind, we can also know that there is forgiveness when we stumble, and our children are always there waiting to receive our love and attention when we try again to be more present with them.

Love is a complex thing, isn't it? We just discussed a commonality amongst children of needing the time and attention of their parents to feel loved, but there isn't one single action that is definitely loving all of the time. Love changes how it manifests itself according to what is appropriate and needed in any given situation. This is why even giving our child our full attention is not *always* the loving thing to do. If we're on the phone, for example, giving our children our full time and attention would be inappropriate and unloving unless it's an emergency. Unloving to whom? Both our child and the person on the phone. It would be rude to the person on the phone and selfish of our child to demand it. Therefore, giving them time and attention in that moment would be unloving. At that time, teaching the child to be self-less and wait patiently is what is most loving. They must learn to care more about other people than their own immediate desires.

Now let's move to the roof of our house. As you may have noticed, in the description of love, Paul writes, "It [love] always protects." That is the roof of your house. Your protection is what keeps the contents of the house safe from the elements. Your protection over your children is a special assignment that God gave to you and only you when He blessed you with that child. Love always protects. So, when you hear the all-too-common accusation, "*You don't want to be an over-protective parent!,*" remember that, in fact, love always protects. God has said so. We should always protect our children because children desperately need our protection, and because that is what love does. We do so not just from physical dangers but from the even more insidious emotional and spiritual threats as well. Protection does not mean you can shield your children from all evil, of course, as that is impossible. Those who claim this is our intention are creating a straw man against this argument. It's as though you told your child not to jump off a cliff, and someone responded by accusing you of trying to keep your child from experiencing gravity. Not only is that a ridiculous assertion and clearly impossible even if you wanted to, but it is not at all what you are trying to do. You are keeping your child from harm because it is obvious that they will get hurt if they do that. You are, in fact, being loving.

Saying that a child should not jump off a cliff is to be reasonable and intelligent about their safety. It is, in fact, a way to protect them from harming themselves. Similarly, evil is so pervasive that even your own flesh is filled with it, and like gravity, it will be felt no matter what you do. Your child will encounter evil and sin from the moment they are born; in fact, they experience it from conception.[7] It is foolish to think that even the most aware and active parent could shield their child from all the evil in this world. Therefore, those who seem worried that children of protective parents will somehow be unaware of what evil is can just relax. It isn't possible. Those children will be exposed to plenty of evil and sin on a daily basis, and just because your child must confront certain sinful realities at some point does not mean they need to face all of them in any order or at any age.

Children are extremely vulnerable, trusting, and easily influenced by nature. Therefore, it is our job as parents to protect them from the

7. Ps 51:5.

evils we *can* protect them from and to simultaneously guide them in their understanding of wickedness. We are responsible for teaching them how to respond so they can grow in wisdom and virtue. Our protection and guidance evolve over time, developing from birth until they reach eighteen years old.

As they grow, our protection shifts from being entirely on our shoulders to teaching our children how to protect themselves as well. We never abandon the responsibility of protecting them when it is in our power to do so, and when they are unable or unaware enough to do it on their own (just as God does not forsake protecting us when we need it). However, our goal is to equip children with the tools they can use themselves, so they are prepared to enter the outside world.

One way to protect our children is to inoculate them as best we can against various types of evil. What do I mean by this? We can introduce elements of this world a little at a time, coaching them through the process of interacting with difficult concepts that seek to threaten them in some way. A great example of this comes from the issue of transgenderism. I do not expose my kids to transgenderism when they are very, very little and unable to comprehend what is happening. Doing so would only create confusion. However, we do talk about male and female, discussing their differences and that they are made in the image of God. This lays the foundation for future discussions. As they grow, I introduce them to the topic of transgenderism so they can understand the concept from the perspective of God's Word and reality, rather than first experiencing it on the world's terms with all the accolades and appealing glitz and glam that typically accompany this ideology.

When my children are old enough (somewhere around seven years old or so), I show them a video of a transgender child. The clip I have chosen is of a boy dressed as a girl who is being interviewed by a talk show. Before showing them the clip, I explain what will happen. I inform them that the boy will come onto the stage and receive a lot of applause and compliments. The crowd will cheer for him. This boy will be told that he is bold and fierce for dressing up as a girl. Everyone will act as if he has done something wonderful and extraordinary. The boy's parents will also be present, and they will be praised for their "accepting" parenting and acknowledged for being loving because they participate in this charade with their child.

The family will be portrayed as the ideal family and displayed for others to follow their example. I then show them the interview. Why do I do this? Because I believe in the power of inoculation. Showing our children, when appropriate, what they will encounter in this world better prepares them to stand strong against it all. They will not be caught off guard, nor will they be confused when they see many people responding so positively to things that they have been taught are wrong.

I chose this tactic because years ago I was sitting in a dentist's office waiting for my appointment when this very same interview came on the TV. I almost always had my children with me at my appointments, but this time I did not. I realized how detrimental it would have been for them to see transgenderism for the very first time in such an extremely positive light. Everyone was oohing and ahhing at this boy dressed as a girl, creating such an ecstatic scene that it looked like a very desirable achievement indeed. They would have heard that parents who go along with this are good parents, and everyone seemed to agree with that. We had never talked about it before then, and they did not know anything about it at the time. If I had prepared them, I knew it would have less effect and impact.

Inoculation, as it were, is not the only way to protect our children. There are obvious physical protections we employ when our children are young, and the question is, how do we address this issue of protection as they grow older? We can use violence as an example and begin in early childhood. Let's say you have a baby who is crawling around on the floor, and another kid comes over in a fit of anger and pushes your baby backwards, causing them to smack their head on the floor. Do you (a) rush over and protect your baby from further violence or (b) stand there and see if your baby protects themselves? Of course, you rush over and protect your child. Why? Because they need you to do that. They are inexperienced, weak, and vulnerable. They do not know how to defend themselves, nor do they have the strength to defend themselves if they did know how.

As they grow, you teach your young child how to respond to violence by demonstrating appropriate reactions when your child faces harm. You establish clear boundaries with other children when necessary and communicate basic behavioral expectations for your child and others when required. You can also discuss your child's experiences afterward, using their natural interactions as valuable learning opportunities.

As your child continues to grow, you can discuss how to identify healthy friendships so they are drawn to people who foster potentially good relationships while also providing warning signs for unhealthy relationships.

Protection takes various forms and modalities as children grow and develop, but it is always an essential part of parenting. Childhood is a time of immense growth in wisdom and understanding, and children need training and guidance throughout their development. That is one reason God gave them parents! All of this is part of protection.

As we conclude our discussion of the framework we are developing in early childhood, we want to remind ourselves to remain focused as Christian parents. Our focus is on Christ. That is where we want to train our children's eyes to be as well. The entire framework of our house, built on the solid foundation of God's Word, is designed to support and encourage our children towards a strong faith in their Lord and Savior, Jesus Christ. Every element of our house has this singular goal in mind. The Lord has called us to this good purpose, and He is faithful.

9

Starting Down the Education Route

Introducing the Three Primary Skill sets

I NEVER EXPECTED MY educational journey to take this path. I had experienced a variety of school systems and had been a teacher in the public schools, so I simply assumed that education was pretty straightforward and self-explanatory—that it was, essentially, what I had already experienced. There didn't seem to be many different options available, fundamentally speaking. I figured it was six of one, half a dozen of the other when it came to curricula—whether that was in school or at home. Additionally, there were many things I had accepted about children—how they learn and their capabilities and limitations—that I had not actually verified myself.

The most eye-opening experience for me—the point at which my entire viewpoint shifted—was when my children learned how to read. That experience was such a monumental shift that it opened my eyes to children's limitless capabilities. It was astounding to see how much they retained and how capable they were. It also made me realize how terribly low the bar is set at school and even at home regarding learning. There is so much misinformation out there about what we can (and should) do with our young children.

By journeying down this path of homeschooling our children, we discovered that teaching the three primary skill sets (reading, writing, and math) separately is much easier. This makes perfect sense. Difficult skills are easier to learn if you can dedicate yourself solely to the process. For instance, would you find it easier to learn Chinese, Hebrew, and Greek all at the same time, or would you find it easier to learn them one at a time, mastering each before moving on to the next? The question is not what is *possible*, but what is ideal. Ideally, you would learn them sequentially. The same applies to children learning to read, write, and do math. It is possible to learn all three simultaneously, but it is not ideal. We chose to focus on reading first because very young children often struggle with the fine motor skills required for holding a pencil, and naturally, you cannot teach math if they are not yet prepared to hold a pencil. Once reading was more or less mastered, we introduced writing, at which point the children were old enough to hold a pencil correctly. After their handwriting was well established, we added math. This approach worked very well for all of our children.

I will pause here to emphasize that while all three of these primary skills are best taught and learned on an individual basis within the home, this is particularly true for writing. Writing must initially be taught one-on-one to be learned correctly. Even if you plan to send your child to school, prioritizing this skill set before your child leaves home is critical. A child needs constant, individualized oversight as they learn to hold a pencil and form their letters. This oversight can last for months. Even when I believed my child's handwriting was well established, I quickly learned that I still needed to pay close attention. It takes longer than you might think! A child requires consistent reminders on how to form their letters and hold their pencil. Otherwise, bad habits and poor pencil grips can quickly creep in, making future writing not only more challenging and potentially painful but also making cursive a more difficult skill than it needs to be later on. Learning to write well, to form printed letters similarly to cursive, and to hold a pencil comfortably are all skills that will benefit them for the rest of their lives. Once writing is learned, it is almost impossible to unlearn. In other words, it is much easier to teach a child to do this correctly from the beginning than it is to try to undo bad habits later on.

Once the three primary skill sets are firmly established, the floodgates open, allowing the other subjects to fall into place much more easily and quickly. In modern education, the approach is to wait until a child reaches a certain age and then plunge them into the water by teaching them all three major skills simultaneously. The result is that some kids drown, and some barely make it out. It is very difficult to excel with that approach—and how overwhelming it must be for a child!

We will begin with our first primary skill: reading. Teaching children to read at a young age offers numerous benefits beyond the obvious ones. It makes life easier in a variety of ways. First, since reading is no longer a task, your child can concentrate on understanding and following their school instructions instead of on sounding out words. This fosters more independence with schoolwork, as they won't have to wait for you or their teacher to understand what to do, which is empowering for them and freeing for everyone else.

Secondly, children must practice self-discipline and self-control while learning to read; therefore, when it comes time to introduce additional skills and subjects that require the same application, it feels much more natural to them and is seen as an expected part of the process. By the time other subjects are added, it has become standard practice for them to sit and do schoolwork, which they will view as simply part of their routine. They will be eager to incorporate more skills into their repertoire, and that positive outlook on school becomes woven into the culture of your home life.

The reading process also helped our children tackle certain challenges they personally faced. As mentioned previously, our second daughter had a speech impediment caused by chronic ear infections, making reading aloud particularly difficult. Many times during her learning-to-read journey, it was a real battle for (and with) her. She struggled to make the sounds correctly, which was frustrating for her. Part of her challenge stemmed from her stubbornness and pride as well. She disliked being told what to do and felt resentful about not being able to do it well right away. However, we took that in stride as an important issue to address sooner rather than later. Persistence in working with her really paid off. Her pronunciation wasn't always perfect, but it significantly improved over time. Once reading clicked, there was no holding her back, and she continues to read aloud to her youngest sister daily. She finds it hard to believe how difficult the process was for her, but I can certainly remember!

We have another child, Mary, who didn't really speak for the first three years of her life. She made various sounds and communicated well within the family by combining them with gestures. She appeared to be an extremely happy and contented child and not nearly as frustrated at her lack of verbal skills as I was. However, by the time she turned three, I was at a loss. Was she not speaking because her sisters talked constantly? Was she not speaking because she couldn't form the words? Was there something wrong with her? How could I help her? I consulted a speech therapist, and we tried to determine what to do, but the problem was that Mary was far too shy to work with a therapist.

Finally, I decided to use the reading book as a form of speech therapy. I pointed to a letter and asked Mary to repeat the sound. She did. We moved on to the next letter in the book, and I asked her to try another sound. She did it again, perfectly. And so, we slowly proceeded through the lessons. After a few weeks of working through the book, I heard her speak her very first sentence, which was one she read aloud. I cried tears of relief and joy. I was over the moon! I had waited so long to hear her sweet voice articulate words, and I had felt that day would never come. Eventually, she completed the reading book, and now she has joined her sisters in talking all the time.

My point is to encourage you that your child *can* do this. While it will be difficult and they will present their own unique set of challenges to you, there is a tremendous reward at the end, and the benefits are simply too numerous to list.

Now the big question: How do you teach reading? Simple! You find a phonics program and teach a little bit every day. I personally have used a book called *Teach Your Child to Read in 100 Easy Lessons*, and I would recommend it for its ease and affordability. It is a single, easy-to-use book, which is nice instead of having to buy multiple books or purchase a variety of materials. In that one book, they tell you exactly what to say and what to do. It is basically foolproof since none of it is left for you to figure out. The book ends at a second grade reading level. There are many other options available for parents, and it's best to pick one and start!

There are a few things to remember when teaching reading. The first is that your child is not too young to start. If they can point to a picture of a cow and say "moo," then they can point to an A and say "ah." You do not need to teach them the alphabet first. Some of my children knew their alphabet letter names first, and some did not. It made no real difference. The point is to just start learning how to make the sounds on the page.

A very important thing to remember when teaching reading is that *it takes time*. Many parents do not see improvement within an arbitrary time frame, and therefore, they can become discouraged. They might also find it challenging to teach their child to sit and focus, and so they mistakenly believe that their child is not ready to learn to read. This is simply not true. Children cannot learn to read overnight, nor can they develop the self-discipline required to sit for a short time and follow instructions without being taught to do so. Both of these things require time, teaching, and persistence!

A child's brain simply cannot learn a major skill like reading quickly, and there are reasons for this. The brain undergoes physical changes as a child learns to read. The National Institutes of Health published a study explaining that "reading requires efficient communication between brain regions that are situated all over the cortex. These brain areas are structurally connected by white-matter pathways that develop over the period of reading acquisition."[1] The development of these white matter pathways is a significant process and involves networks in the brain used for language, vision, and attention.

The brain's white matter pathways are formed by the axons of neurons.[2] Neurons serve as information messengers in the brain, and each one has a tail called an axon. Signals (a.k.a. information) are transmitted from one neuron down the axon to another neuron. Axons must grow and connect to facilitate this transmission. In addition, myelin is produced in the brain during learning. Myelin consists of protein and fatty substances, providing insulation for the axons.

Myelin is like the plastic coating on the wires in your home, serving a similar purpose: it insulates the wires and prevents electrical signals from leaking out of one wire (or axon) into another. Myelin naturally begins in utero (around sixteen weeks' gestation) and continues through adulthood, with an overall increase by two years of age. However, myelin is also produced through certain activities and is "highly sensitive to environmental factors,"[3] and, therefore, myelin directly increases according to learning-related activities.[4] Myelin also speeds up signals from one neuron to another. An unmyelinated axon sends signals at about 0.5 to 10 meters per second (m/s), whereas a myelinated axon can send signals at velocities up to 150 m/s.[5] (This means it is up to 300 times faster when there is myelin on

1. Cheema and Cummine, "Relationship Between White Matter," 1.

2. The reason white matter is called "white" is because of the myelin, which is fatty and thus produces that coloration in the brain.

3. Hutton et al., "Associations Between Screen-Based Media Use," 174.

4. Forbes and Gallo, "All Wrapped Up," 572–87.

5. Purves et al., "Increased Conduction Velocity."

the axon!) A thicker myelin sheath enhances all types of cognitive tasks and is also linked with better decision-making!

A study funded by the Cincinnati Children's Research Foundation found that, "While reading can be acquired at any age, this process is *most efficient* during the span of maximal brain plasticity in early childhood."[6] Early childhood is defined in this study as "preschool age children" (between 3–4 years old). This supports the fact that the earlier you provide your child with the incredible gift of reading, the better.

Add to this a fascinating study conducted by researchers at Emory University in 2014 that used MRIs to examine changes in resting-state brain connectivity among college students who had read a novel. The study discovered clearly defined heightened connectivity in the brain for several days after reading a novel.[7] Reading not only significantly develops white matter pathways in the brain and accelerates information processing time, but it also heightens connectivity between brain regions on both a short-term and long-term developmental basis.

At this point, if you've managed to get through all that scientific jargon without throwing the book away, you might want to shout at this page, "*Why are you telling me this?*" And I'll explain why: because it matters. Understanding this helps you persist as your child learns to read. The brain undergoes significant physical growth and changes when a child masters this crucial skill. This growth unfolds naturally and gradually *over time*. In scientific terms, this learning process is called "productive struggle." Productive struggle occurs when someone grapples with information somewhat above their current ability and persists in this struggle over time, eventually obtaining mastery. This engagement allows changes in their brain to take place. It is only through this process that a child will experience that "ah-ha" moment when the concept clicks, resulting in a breakthrough in learning. This is why determination and consistency are essential.

Children who learn to read at a young age progress much more easily and quickly in their studies and their general knowledge of the world. They can pick up books on any topic that interests them and learn. Children gain far more knowledge this way than you or I could ever teach them.

We have countless books, children's encyclopedias, and various informational literature lying around the house. Our children have found endless entertainment, inspiration, and knowledge within them. My kids are always

6. Hutton et al., "Associations Between Home Literacy Environment," 1.
7. Berns et al., "Short- and Long-Term Effects," 590–600 (emphasis added).

sharing new things they've learned through their independent reading, and I end up learning so much from them! Reading aligns perfectly with how children are created, into their curiosity and their need to ask a billion questions. In books, they can explore the world and find answers. Reading beautifully satisfies the almost insatiable desire that children have to *know*. It is an incredible blessing, and I often say it's the most important thing a parent can teach their children besides faith in God. Reading opens up the entire world to a child *for life*, and it is a gift worth pursuing.

10

Tips for Teaching Reading

MANY PARENTS FIND TEACHING reading to be a daunting task. Our culture strongly emphasizes "experts" in general and suggests that only they are qualified to teach. As ordinary parents, we may feel that we are not competent enough to undertake something so important. We haven't received a certificate from any organization that deems us capable. Some parents may feel so overwhelmed by the prospect of teaching this skill that they send their child to school to learn to read, planning to withdraw them later in order to educate them at home. This may seem illogical, but it simply reflects the impact that the "expert" ideology has had on parents' mentality.

Teaching reading isn't as complicated as you might think. You don't need to be an "expert." There are many programs and books available to guide you and your child through the process successfully. Regardless of who you are or what your background is, you *can* do it. Below are some tips and tricks you may find useful as you navigate the process. Remember, you *and* your child are capable!

- Start early in the day.

Starting right after breakfast with a short reading lesson has been the most successful method I have found for ensuring we meet our goal of reading a little every day. If I wait until later in the day, not only is my child less focused, but it's also easier to get busy and forget to do it. Habits are easiest to form if you can ensure consistency through routine, and the first thing in the morning is the simplest way to establish that routine. Since we have multiple children, we've had to ensure that the older kids understand that whoever is learning to read takes precedence over everything else. We hold this time as almost sacred in our family. The child who is learning to read gets our complete focus after breakfast, and the older children must wait for their needs and questions until the youngest child has completed their reading lesson.

- Offer small immediate rewards (M&Ms, mini chocolate chips, small marshmallows).

  Low/no sugar options: Quest Peanut Butter Cups (cut up), pretzels, gummy snacks, berries, stickers.

Children respond well to a small reward when they are tackling this new and all-important skill of learning to read. This is not for compliance, however. When a child is asked to complete a task, they need to do it regardless of a reward, as this helps them practice obedience. The treat was there to excite them, creating an association in their mind between working hard and joy. This positive connection is really helpful during the reading process. To support this, I found it essential not to offer sugar at any other time during the day, so the child would look forward to a treat. The treat was always given once the child accomplished the task, no matter how small or large, and the one rule was that they could only earn the treat if they *also* had a good attitude during the assignment. They could not receive a reward if they were doing their work with a sour face or whiny voice.

When they were first learning to read—the initial few lessons—they received a very small reward (such as a mini-M&M or a mini-marshmallow) for every word they sounded out. Once we moved on to short stories, they would not receive a treat after every word, but rather they would earn treats after each sentence. After we progressed to longer stories, they would only get a small handful of chocolates after finishing the entire story. Eventually, we completely weaned off the treats, and surprisingly, not one of the children ever even noticed, something I would not have believed possible earlier in the process! By the end of the book, each child had found such success and joy in reading, as they could engage with the material instead of being bogged down by the tediousness of sounding out words, that the candy was forgotten without any battles at all.

During this initial stage of the reading process, we are teaching children to do what they do not want to do when they need to. They have never had to apply themselves to something in quite this way before. Thus, we provide a reward for conquering this internal battle: they may not feel like completing the task before them, but they do it anyway, and as a result, they experience joy. That is the lesson. As they learn more and more, the *joy of learning* becomes a legitimate and meaningful reward.

- Establish a long-term-goal reward!

Whenever one of our children started the reading book, we talked with them about the incredible opportunity they were being given. "*You are going to learn to read!* Can you believe it? You'll be able to read whatever you want, whenever you want! You'll be just like mommy and daddy!" We also told them what we would do as a family once they finished the book. For all our kids, we told them that we would go out and celebrate, whether it was ice cream or a dinner out. We chose something we knew would really excite them. You can choose any reward you want for your children. Maybe a trip to see Grandma and Grandpa, getting a cake from the grocery store, buying them a toy they want, going to a trampoline park, or taking a trip to an amusement park. The options are limitless. You know what makes your kid tick, so pinpoint that and make the reward something that communicates what a big deal this really is.

When your child finishes the book, they will be prepared to read and tackle other learning for the rest of their lives. Build it up for them, then, because otherwise, how will they understand how important this really is? Children cannot view the future in the same way adults do. They are unlikely to feel excited and motivated every day simply by knowing that eventually they will learn how to read. Therefore, we can supplement that excitement for a while with a tactile reward they can look forward to until they achieve what they've set out to accomplish. Once they finish the book, the reward will simply be icing on the cake for them. They will then understand the significance of this skill and appreciate what a great accomplishment it is. They will burst with pride and excitement about their abilities. However, at the beginning of the book, they have not reached that point and cannot fully grasp it, so we help them feel motivated and enthusiastic by providing a meaningful reward to anticipate.

- Ensure a quiet environment.

A quiet environment is important for a child's focus, especially when the task is challenging for them to master. Turn off all music, set aside your phone, and use a sound machine if necessary. Remove yourself and your child from all distractions. Their reading time must be quiet. Go into a room and close the door, or have other children go somewhere they cannot be heard for a short time. Learning to read is a gigantic and complex skill for a child. Protect their learning time diligently and honor their need for quiet so they can concentrate.

- Praise!

I am a strong believer in offering ample praise because it is deserved when children undertake the challenging task of learning to read. When my children began learning to read and produced even one correct sound, I praised them enthusiastically for it. Children need the verbal approval and encouragement of their parents. This is crucial for their hearts. This really is a big deal and quite challenging for them, and the only way they will understand how much you appreciate their hard work is through clear communication.

- Don't be afraid to help them and keep the pace up!

When I started teaching my first child to read, I thought I couldn't help her sound out words, or she wouldn't remember those sounds on her own. To me, it seemed equivalent to telling a child the answer to a math problem. How would they know how to do it the next time on their own? However, I have discovered that this is not at all how reading works. Helping a child who is struggling to remember a certain sound, even when they should (in your mind) know that sound by now, is beneficial for them. Give them a chance to figure it out for themselves first, and then remind them if necessary. It's important to keep the pace up so that reading doesn't become horrible drudgery. One word should not take five whole minutes for your child to figure out.

- Cover the picture.

Depending on the program used, pictures will often accompany the stories. Parents may think that colorful pictures will enhance the reading process. To a certain extent, this is true, but it's beneficial to cover the picture while your child is figuring out the sounds. Otherwise, children may spend an excessive amount of time looking at the image instead of focusing on the words. Even after studying the picture, their eyes will inevitably drift back to it while reading the story. This makes it difficult for them to maintain focus, and they lose track of where they are in the story, which leads to guessing at words based on the picture. It's much easier for a child to concentrate on sounding out words and understanding the story without the picture, and then they can view the image afterward as a type of additional reward.

- When working on only individual words, make up sentences to fit the word.

When learning to read, you always start with individual words, not with stories. To provide those words with context in the real world, I found it very beneficial to quickly create a sentence for each word. For example, if my child sounded out the word "pan," I might say, "I need a *pan* to cook with. *Pan*." This approach helps a child understand how the word functions within a sentence. It essentially brings the word to life.

- If needed, you can break up the lesson throughout the day.

Some days, a child has more focus than on others. Within reason and using your own judgment, we can conform to those needs. The caveat here is not to mistake a child's *unwillingness* to do something for their *inability* to do something. Parents need to pay close attention to their children to determine if they are truly unable to focus or if they simply don't want to sit and do the lesson. Early on in this process, I break up the lessons much more readily than later on, as their attention span grows and it is less taxing on their young minds to complete the assignments. You should expect a trajectory over time that shows an increase in the amount of time you can spend on the reading lesson for the day. Test the waters every so often. Add a little extra on a day when things have been going smoothly. Think of it like working out—the more you do it, the stronger you become and the more you can add to your routine. The same is true for reading. You are exercising their minds, and therefore, you can expect to see overall growth in their attention span. At the beginning, however, you may need to break up your lessons into smaller chunks.

- It's OK to go back and review the same lesson the next day.

There is no exact schedule for learning to read. The goal is *not* merely to move from lesson to lesson so you can complete the program; rather, the objective is to learn to read! If a child truly needs to go back and review a lesson, go for it. However, I would not recommend doing that frequently, as it might discourage your student from feeling as though they are not making progress. Thankfully, most of the time, the concepts from one lesson will reappear in the next for additional practice, making repetition of one particular lesson often unnecessary. Still, if you believe it is necessary, taking a day to review a lesson can be beneficial.

- Use a pencil to point *above* the word as your child points their finger underneath it.

What does this mean? A child will point to each sound as they say it in a word. I hold a pencil over the top of the word and drag it along to help their eyes glide over it. This encourages them to view the word as a whole, rather than just looking at one letter at a time. A child's tendency is to see individual letters vertically instead of horizontally, as if each letter is a word unto itself. We want to encourage their eyes to look toward the end of the word, even when they are at the beginning of it. This will help them to identify words faster and more easily in the future.

- Ensure they are connecting the sounds as much as possible.

Ideally, a child connects each sound in a word to the next sound of that same word. Many children, including my own, struggle with this at first. They tend to articulate one sound, pause, and then say the next sound. This pattern continues until the end of the word, which makes it difficult for them to perceive the word as a whole. While this isn't a major concern, it is helpful to encourage your child to link each sound in the word to the following one.

- Keep reminding them to read sounds they *see*, not sounds they *think*!

I regularly remind my children to read the sounds they *see*, not the sounds they *think they know*. This is similar to what we discussed earlier about covering a picture to prevent word guessing, but it is actually a different issue. When children look at a picture, they might guess completely random words that have no relation to the sounds in front of them. However, when a child is simply reading new words, their brain may attempt to guess words they already know that share some of those same letters. They need reminding to adhere to the written words. They cannot make things up or guess. It's helpful to encourage them to say whatever sounds are present, even if they have no idea what the word is or what it means. Nine times out of ten, they will recognize the word after they have sounded it out.

- Make sure when they sound out a word, they repeat it back *fast*.

Children learning to read can take quite a bit of time to sound words out, especially at the beginning of the reading process. We need to allow for that time (while ensuring they don't get bogged down too deeply in the process), and then we need to remind them to repeat the word quickly after they finish. In the beginning, I typically repeat the word for the child, but later on, I have them repeat the word "the fast way" for themselves. For example, a child may sound out the word "ran" like this: "rrrrrrrraaaaaaaaannnnnn." So, I will ask them to say it the fast way and they will say simply "ran."

- Reread sentences after the child reads them, and do so in an engaging way.

As a child reads their sentences, we must remember that their pace will inevitably be somewhat slow. I found that it helps to maintain their engagement in the story if, after every word, I quickly repeat the sentence, using a voice that shows investment in what we are reading. This may sound excessive, but once you listen to their pace, you will understand why it is definitely not! I make sure my voice is animated and excited, not dull and blasé. I don't want to bore them to death. I want them to engage with the written word. Rereading the sentences keeps them on track with the story.

- When transitioning to sounding words out in silence, have them speak it quietly so that you can't hear them . . . like a secret!

Once you are further along in the process, you may reach a point where you feel your child is ready to think the sounds in their head instead of sounding everything out audibly. To transition into this, I encourage my children to whisper the sounds very, very softly, as if it's a tremendous secret. So softly, in fact, that I can't hear them. I am sitting right next to them and have a mother's hearing, so they really must be very quiet! It doesn't take too long for very quiet whispering to become mouthing, which transitions later into silence. As always, this will only happen with your persistence and guidance.

- "Code letters."

Code letters are used in phonics programs to provide children with a visual representation of the different sounds that one or two letters can create. A phonics program may combine sounds like "th," "ch," and "ea," physically connecting the letters. When we wean off those visual cues, I remind my child of what they are by often circling them on the paper and saying things like, "Ch goes together and it says 'ch!'" Before too long, my child hears my voice in their head, repeating the rules I've been teaching them, making circling no longer necessary.

- It is important to pick literature that they can succeed at.

When learning to read, I do not encourage my child to read any book other than the one we are using to develop this valuable new skill. They are free to flip through various books, and they have books read to them on a daily basis, but I don't have them read outside of our lesson book. This is because it is far too easy to confuse them with different reading strategies, and it can also discourage and frustrate a child if you introduce material that is too difficult for them at these early stages. Sticking with our reading program ensures we are providing material that matches their ability level.

Help your child prepare to tackle outside books by completing their reading program first. Then, introduce literature at a level you believe they can succeed with. At the back of this book, I've included a list of the books we use at home, organized by increasing difficulty, which may assist you with this challenge. For some children, there is a period of disbelief in their ability to read outside books. They need to "see it to believe it." For a child who has never picked up a book to successfully read it independently, the experience can feel surreal and may take time for them to believe in themselves. That is why success in the early stages is so important. We want to present material that they can manage without too much difficulty to help build their confidence. Once their confidence is high, you can begin to challenge them with more difficult literature.

Teaching your child to read is the biggest challenge you'll face in their early childhood education. However, once you climb that mountain, step by step, the rest will fall into place much more easily. Remember: focus on one major skill at a time during early childhood. Before you know it, your child will be meeting goals and exceeding expectations!

11

Discovering the Old to Reveal Something New

A Look into Classical Education

THERE ARE TWO PRIMARY philosophical systems that influence most of our current educational choices in America. These systems serve as the foundation for the majority of curriculum options available today, and they represent either a modern or a classical approach. The choice between them will largely dictate everything from what your child learns to how they will learn it. Public schools, of course, provide only a modern education. Most institutions will offer some variation of the same. Depending on your location, you may find a classical school. These are typically private institutions, often affiliated with a church. Homeschool programs provide both options. It is essential to understand the origins of these two mainstream philosophies and the theories they embrace in order to choose the best option for your child and their future.

We will start with a classical education. What is classical education? Classical education is a system of education that dates back to almost 400 BC with Aristotle. Aristotle was a prominent Greek philosopher who believed that education is a lifelong pursuit that should cultivate intellectual and moral virtue. What does that mean? It means that there is truth, and we should seek it in our studies. There is truth about the physical universe, there is truth about right behavior, there is truth about the impacts and merits of civilizations and governments, and there is a shared gift among humans of reason, which allows us to pursue these truths in communion with one another. This means we can debate and reason with one another to arrive at the truth. This type of education is specifically for those concerned with the study of wisdom. Things are not to be studied solely for practical application or an end goal, but for an understanding of our universe. This is a fundamental aspect of a classical education. It is for the sake of learning and not for the sake of specific grades or the end goal of a job alone. Education isn't, in other words, just a means to an end. It is good in itself. An education is worthwhile *because it is an education*, and those who embrace a classical viewpoint believe that gaining wisdom and virtue is a beneficial activity for all human beings.

This educational system is based on a framework called the Trivium. The Trivium is a Latin term meaning "three ways." It consists of Grammar, Logic, and Rhetoric. These three stages align with a child's natural intellectual growth process as they develop and capitalizes on their gifts and tendencies at their various ages and in their various stages of development.

Dorothy Sayers, who lived in the early 1900s, was a brilliant, witty, and prolific Christian writer. She was also one of the first women to graduate with an earned degree from Oxford University and was a friend of C. S. Lewis.[1] She was a staunch advocate of a classical education. She wrote a short but poignant essay called "The Lost Tools of Learning," in which she brilliantly presents her arguments in favor of a classical education. In this book, she explains that the Trivium is meant "to teach a pupil the proper use of the tools of learning, before he begins to apply them to 'subjects' at all."[2] She argues that the Trivium is, by its nature, the *preparation for learning*, and therefore, we cannot start children too young. I completely agree! Classical education focuses on the capabilities of children and taps into their very real and present potential by inspiring and challenging every child at every age. Thus, efforts are made even when children are very young to equip them for their lifelong pursuit of knowledge and virtue.

Referring to the Trivium as preparation for learning does not imply that we do not learn subjects within it. We certainly do. However, it is important to emphasize that the Trivium is not *solely* about what students

---

1. Their correspondence is recorded in *Dorothy and Jack: The Transforming Friendship of Dorothy L. Sayers and C. S. Lewis* by Gina Dalfonzo.

2. Sayers, *Lost Tools*, 14.

learn in K–12 grades. In fact, the Trivium forms the basis for how students will learn all things *in the future*. It is a system of learning. They will go through the Trivium as adults. At various points in their lives, when they want to learn about any topic of their choosing, they will utilize elements of the Trivium to pursue that knowledge.

There may also be instances when they need to revisit a particular stage on a topic they already know much about. For example, if they are studying a language and discover they do not fully grasp conjugations, they might need to return to the grammar stage to memorize more about them. Or perhaps in a discussion at college, they realize they do not completely understand why a historical event occurred; in that case, they could revisit the logic stage. They will know how to approach these problems precisely because they have received a classical education and can apply the methodologies that they have become accustomed to.

The Trivium also offers a broad foundation of concrete knowledge to build upon throughout a child's future. By memorizing extensive amounts of information during the original grammar stage, students are poised to add easily and naturally to their foundational knowledge in later years. This knowledge fits together like interlocking wood, building a secure framework of connected understanding about the world and the universe. The Trivium not only equips you with tools for learning, but it has historically emphasized the content of what you study. A classical education enhances your understanding of the world in solid, factual ways, directly linking new information to prior knowledge.

The grammar stage is the first stage, lasting from as early as possible until the logic stage, which typically begins around the fourth grade nowadays. It's important to clarify that the grammar stage does not end at the logic stage; rather, it transitions into it. When the term "grammar" is used in relation to the grammar stage, it encompasses more than just syntax and spelling. It is a broad term that refers to foundational knowledge gained primarily through memorization. Just as the small "g" grammar serves as the foundation of language, so the grammar stage acts as the foundation of learning. Children memorize many things in this stage, and they will then use this knowledge in more critical and rational ways as they develop through the other stages. In this stage, they are gathering the facts and storing them away for future use.

Children at this age easily memorize things, as I say, and find great joy in doing so. In this stage, they quickly memorize rules of grammar, spelling, writing, historical events and dates, vocabulary in English and foreign languages, math facts, etc. They thrive on memorization. They enjoy spouting off what they've learned and pointing out their knowledge of the world around them. They are not reflecting on their feelings about these subjects or asking critical thinking questions, but rather absorbing information and retaining it.

Logic (the next stage in the Trivium) is the art of thinking, typically occurring around the fourth grade and continuing until about the seventh or eighth grade. This is the combative stage. As Dorothy Sayers put it, "It is difficult to say at what age, precisely, we should pass from the first to the second part of the Trivium. Generally speaking, the answer is: as soon as the pupil shows himself disposed to pertness and interminable argument."[3] She categorizes the three stages of the Trivium this way: the Poll-Parrot stage, the Pert stage, and the Poetic stage. These are apt descriptions: Poll-Parrot (they like to repeat and memorize), Pert (they are impertinent and question everything), and the Poetic (they reflect on the world around them and on themselves). She writes about the Pert stage: "It will, doubtless, be objected that to encourage young persons at the Pert Age to browbeat, correct, and argue with their elders will render them perfectly intolerable. My answer is that children of that age are intolerable anyhow; and that their natural argumentativeness may just as well be channeled to good purpose as allowed to run away into the sands."[4]

This is very true. Your child will enter this stage with or without your guidance and assistance in how to use their inclinations to do battle for good. It's our opportunity to train their minds to think critically, to question things, and to use logic and factual knowledge to ferret out the truth. This stage provides a fantastic opportunity to equip their young minds to face the onslaught of the outside world. We live in the age of information, and children need to know how to sift through that information, to think critically about it, and to form their own conclusions (not to merely adopt other people's conclusions!). It is more important than ever to teach our children how to think and reason so they can navigate through the ideologies and falsehoods in the world to find truth in all areas of life.

We continue to teach subjects in the logic stage, but we view our specific subjects differently. All subjects are a subdepartment, or branch, of logic, rather than separate, individual subjects. This part of the logic

3. Sayers, *Lost Tools*, 28.
4. Sayers, *Lost Tools*, 33.

stage represents simply a difference in perspective, but it can make all the difference. For example, instead of viewing history as a segregated subject, we consider history through the lens of our theological knowledge, along with our understanding of logic and science, combining these with the historical facts learned in the grammar stage.

This allows us to ask questions about what we're learning. We are integrating various subjects into each other. Now we can ask questions like whether something was justified or why a battle was lost, tactically speaking. We can present arguments for or against certain types of governments. We can investigate bills in light of other bills that preceded them. We can view scientific discoveries within their historical context. In fact, all the subjects make more sense at this stage because you've learned so much about factual information during the grammar stage. We continue to teach students how to question, how to argue, and how to think. As I mentioned, each stage builds upon the previous one, so the logic stage is not disconnected from the grammar stage. The emphasis is no longer on memorization but on developing logical skills. However, this does not mean you'll never have to memorize anything.

It is as though we made the tools in the grammar stage, and in the logic stage we start having the student pick up the tools to learn how to use them. We guide their hands in their application of these tools, ensuring they are using them as deftly as possible.

The final stage of the Trivium is Rhetoric. Rhetoric is typically taught during the high school years. It is the art of communication that combines logic and grammar. This is the point at which a student begins to express and refine their views based on their knowledge of the world. They have the tools of learning and the art of logic to apply to their own questions and interests. At this stage, they have learned more about how to ferret out information, question assumptions, and connect the dots in their learning. They are still guided by an adult, of course. They are not wandering about on their own. Some argue that this is the stage when children should be given more freedom to specialize, if they show an interest. Let them delve more deeply into a given subject or two, while not forsaking the rest of their learning. Literature will no longer be so destructively criticized as it was during the logic stage; instead, it will be appreciated more, and they can start self-expression in writing. This stage emphasizes persuasive writing and speaking skills, honing originality as students practice weaving together more complex ideas.

There is a second part of a classical education that was historically combined with the Trivium to make up the famous seven liberal arts. This second part is called the Quadrivium, which was used in higher education during the Middle Ages. The term "Quadrivium" means "four ways" and refers to the arts of number, while the Trivium represents the arts of the word. The Quadrivium encompassed four general subject areas: arithmetic, geometry, music, and astronomy. Arithmetic was considered the foundation of the Quadrivium and involved the study of numbers. Geometry focused on forms and shapes of objects and how they interacted with one another (numbers in space). Astronomy concentrated on geometric concepts in space, and music was the combination of sounds as a mathematical science involving intervals and harmony. Historically, the study of the Quadrivium completed one's formal education before one specialized in fields such as medicine or law, for example.

Our focus here is on the Trivium—the idea that it aligns with the natural progression of children's development and can also be applied once your child enters the outside world as a young adult. This system empowers individuals to learn more easily, specialize, investigate, and create. They don't have to wait until adulthood to effectively use their learning tools with great success, either. I told my children recently that if they memorized every country in Africa, they could earn a handful of chocolates. My then-nine-year-old, having a sweet tooth, decided to memorize all the countries. She accomplished this in under an hour. When she came bounding up to tell me all the countries, I asked her how she managed to do it so quickly. She explained that she took four countries at a time, grouping them together to memorize, and once she had learned those, she added another four. She mentioned that this is the same system she uses to memorize her Latin grammar and that she had just applied it to memorizing the countries. She was able to handle such a monumental task efficiently and joyfully.

Sayers predicted just such abilities when she wrote, "For the tools of learning are the same, in any and every subject; and the person who knows how to use them will, at any age, get the mastery of a new subject in half the time and with a quarter of the effort expended by the person who has not the tools at his command. To learn six subjects without remembering how they were learnt does nothing to ease the approach to a seventh; to have learnt and remembered the art of learning makes the approach to every subject an open door."[5] This is one of our main goals as parents. We want our children

5. Sayers, Lost Tools, 38.

to have the tools of learning so that they are enabled to pursue knowledge, as well as their own personal interests, more easily. Their education, therefore, is aimed at equipping them in this pursuit.

12

The Inmates Are Running the Prison

A Look Inside Modern Education

You MAY BE WONDERING how different the classical approach really is from the modern approach to education. Perhaps it is just an issue of personal preference, and it doesn't really matter which one you choose. After all, there are many paths up the same mountain, right?

To answer that question, let's begin with what modern educational philosophy teaches, so we can compare apples to apples. Some commonly used terms you may be familiar with in modern education are "student-centered learning," "active learning," "self-directed learners," "independence," "inclusivity," and "progressivism" (which is the teaching that we need to educate kids in a certain way to produce a certain specific type of society that fits with progressive viewpoints and ideologies).

Modern education is not fundamentally the communication of truth and ideas from the teacher to the student. The teacher strives to be more of a guide, while the student is the real leader in modern education. The teacher must focus on students' desires and engagement, shifting their teaching styles and even their content around what gets the student interested. I saw this up close and personal as a teacher in the public schools. As a teacher, you were responsible for ensuring your students wanted to learn—their feelings about their education were of paramount importance. If they didn't want to learn, it was your fault. You weren't presenting things in an engaging enough way. It wasn't the fault of the program or the curriculum itself. In other words, it wasn't something intrinsically wrong with the hollowness of the content being taught or the test you were preparing the students to take. There was definitely nothing wrong with the fractured nature of their education. No. It was your fault because learning should be fun and exciting . . . always.

Children in modern education should always see the practical use of what they're being taught. Every math problem, for example, should make them see how they can use their math skills in real-world practical applications. You can't expect a child to learn math for the sake of learning the skill of logic and problem-solving.

It is not the child's responsibility to sit there and learn from the teacher, regardless of their feelings. *That* way of teaching may have successfully worked for millions of children across all civilizations in the Western world for literally thousands of years, but children today are totally different, and expectations should be totally different. They cannot learn that way. It was your responsibility to ensure the child *wants* to sit and learn the material at all times. I remember many occasions when the principal or vice principal would sit in on my classes and those of my coworkers, and the main focus was on that aspect of the educational process, not the content of the class.

Children were leading the teachers, in essence. Yes, the teachers still had to prepare students primarily for the tests, but this had to be done in such a way that children felt "empowered" because they felt a sense of control over their education and learning. It is assumed that if children believe they are making their own choices in the learning process, they'll be more inclined to engage with the material. But the dirty little secret is that's not what actually happens. That isn't the actual result. Children are not becoming more engaged with learning through this approach. The truth is that this is failing, and it is doing so in massively obvious ways. Just ask the next kid you see over the age of seven what their favorite subject is, and nine times out of ten, they'll stare at you blankly and say, "I don't know." If you're lucky, they may say, "Recess." This is because, despite all the theatrics and manipulative practices, children are disengaged and uninspired by modern education.

Collaboration is another key component of the modern educational process. Working with one's peers—to determine truth and knowledge—is a highly sought-after good and something that takes up entirely too much of the day in modern education. I quickly learned as a teacher about the high priority that the schools place on collaboration versus teachers actually teaching the material. We're told it is "old school" (and the assumption is that things done in the past are bad by default—which is the logical fallacy of *argumentum ad novitatem*), and therefore it is also "dry" and "boring" for a teacher to stand in front of children and teach.

At this point, it's important to emphasize the need for us to be aware of the potential for word magic during discussions on childhood education. Word magic occurs when words are used to create an unconscious bias against something, not based on facts, but on the basis of negative connotations associated with the language used. This tactic is an all-too-common weapon being wielded today. For instance, calling someone a racist may initially provoke negative reactions from listeners, but that doesn't necessarily mean that person is actually a racist. Similarly, when someone identifies as a boy while being biologically female, it doesn't change their biological status. Claiming something will be boring for kids doesn't make it boring for them. We must seek evidence first, avoiding distractions from the word magic employed, and use that information to either accept or refute the claim. Remember: people often feel intensely about harmful or false things. Their passion doesn't alter reality. Fifty million Frenchmen *can* be wrong!

A basic assumption underlying modern educational philosophy boils down to this: that second graders, for example, are already filled with the ability to determine what's best for themselves, and that they can arrive at the truth essentially for themselves and about the world without too much interference from adults. Interference is bad. Teaching is like a necessary evil; you should try to do as little of it as possible. Get them doing hands-on activities. Does the hands-on activity teach them anything more than what you briefly told them? Who cares! It's a hands-on activity, so it is, by definition, *good*! Remember to focus on making hollow material as exciting as possible—a losing proposition indeed.

There's always a grain of truth in every lie. That's an important thing to recognize as an adult. Lies are not usually completely 100 percent false. There is something about a lie—that grain of truth—that makes it believable in the first place. This grain of truth is that we do hope that our children will be excited and engaged in their education. But you don't get that by aiming at it. You achieve that by teaching children and giving them a rigorous and cohesive education. The by-product of a rigorous and cohesive education is excitement and engagement. It happens naturally with a solid, good, comprehensive education.

In my home state of California, there are many test cases we can examine to view modern educational philosophy reaching its natural, full-blown conclusion within the confines of a single school. In my hometown of Santa Barbara, a school opened up in 2023 called the Santa Barbara Free School.[1] This school implemented the fundamental tenets of a modern education, which center around autonomy, a focus on personal desire, and student control. They boasted of facilitating learning through a "democratic" process. Students spent the first few weeks of school voting and deciding what they wanted to learn and how they wanted to learn it. Do they want a teacher, or do they want to teach themselves? The decision was even in their hands to learn in person or not. What types of activities do they want to engage in? The school used many nice-sounding words, like that it gave "students an opportunity to direct their own learning," and that it was "community-based." It has a "student-led curriculum," and it promises to provide "deep" and "joyous learning."[2] They "mindfully incorporate" skills. And they conclude by claiming that "student-led learning is the future," which is actually the truth amidst the rest of the garbage. This is the natural progression of the view of education so prevalent today. This is where it does actually lead. It comes down to the fact that there is no standard, there is no objective truth, there is only desire and inward turning. You decide what you want to do and how you want to do it as a child—and the adults follow along and supposedly guide you, but do not teach you. So, really, they're there to tell you how wonderful your beliefs and ideas already are. Adults are there to supervise, not to teach truth.

Believe it or not, this school in Santa Barbara boasted that their students would emerge from this program ahead of their peers in their preparation for college. Not surprisingly, this school is temporarily closed, as it lasted only a year. This reflects another common theme in modern educational practices: they're continually changing their teaching practices—trying one thing, finding it ineffective, and then trying another because they are always finding their approaches don't actually work. You can choose any city or town across the US and find a similar outcome. For now, we will continue to focus on my hometown to illustrate this reality in action. In just the last four years (excluding the pandemic years of 2020–22), the

1. Noozhawk, "Santa Barbara Free School's Mission."
2. Indy Parenting Staff, "Education Reimagined."

public schools have experienced eight different curriculum changes and introduced a new type of standardized testing.

Again, change is common within modern education. This is because it fails to produce what many believe it is going to produce. It's like trying to build a house with materials that are not strong enough to support the structure of a house and have not been used to successfully build houses before, so the structure keeps falling apart. Instead of going back to the materials that have proven to be strong enough and sturdy enough to build a house, these individuals continue to insist that in a different combination, the failed materials will surely, someday, make a solid, livable, usable house. And of course, that simply isn't going to happen.

Rather than changing the fundamental philosophies that shape their approach to education and addressing the root of a flawed belief system to create a new foundation, these individuals simply adjust how they implement the ineffective system. So, naturally, it continues to fail!

Another significant test case we can examine to assess the outcomes of modern educational philosophies is found simply by looking at the public schools. Our government has endorsed this form of education for many generations now. Modern educational philosophy developed within the American education system. There is no single curriculum used across every elementary, middle, and high school in America; instead, a diverse range of curricula is applied on a constantly evolving basis, all sharing the same fundamental philosophical perspective. We can see it has failed because we can observe the product of this system.

According to the NAEP (National Assessment of Educational Progress), which tests children in fourth, eighth, and twelfth grades in the public schools, about one-third of children in fourth and eighth grade cannot read at a *basic* level.[3] The most recent NAEP report shows average reading scores for fourth and eighth grade continue to decline and have for over a decade.[4] These tests reveal that 64 percent of fourth graders are *below* proficient in math. According to international standards, 75 percent of eighth graders in America are *below* proficient in math.[5] Forty percent of twelfth graders

---

3. Sparks, "Two Decades of Progress."

4. Sager, "Diving."

5. Both Vivek Ramaswamy and Vice President J. D. Vance have discussed these statistics publicly. For more details, see Lencki, "Vivek Ramaswamy Exposes 'National Security Risk.'"

scored *below* the basic level (a level below proficient and two levels below advanced) in the NAEP math assessment.[6]

Over half (54 percent) of US adults have a literacy level below a sixth-grade standard, and 20 percent read below a fifth-grade level, according to the National Literacy Institute.[7] In the United States, 45 million adults are functionally illiterate.[8] When you look across all grade levels, forty percent of students cannot read at a basic level.[9] Additionally, forty percent of US adults read so poorly that they cannot even read a prescription drug label.[10] To be clear, the overarching illiteracy facts are indeed connected to the modern educational philosophies being implemented in public schools, with 83 percent of US children attending public school, according to Pew Research.[11] Out of the top 38 developed countries worldwide, the United States, which ranks at number one in the world's GDP,[12] plummets to the twenty-sixth spot in terms of education. This means that we have the largest economy in the world, and yet our children are more uneducated than the over two-thirds of the world's most developed countries.

Perhaps at this point, someone might object, arguing that modern educational philosophy can be successfully implemented in a homeschool environment, even if public schools have failed. However, my point is that the public school system has applied modern educational philosophies on a large scale for decades, making it the ideal long-term, extensive, inclusive study to demonstrate results across ethnicities, socioeconomic backgrounds, and age groups. And it has failed. Children today are ignorant, susceptible to ideologies, and unaware of history, broadly speaking. Have you ever seen those interviews on social media where they ask college students basic questions, and they cannot answer them? Questions like how many states are in the United States, or where the Boston Tea Party took place? My personal favorite is when a college student was asked what country the Panama

---

6. This data is from 2019, which is the most recent data available for twelfth grade at the time of this publication. The Nation's Report Card, "National Achievement-Level Results."

7. National Literacy Institute, "Literacy Statistics 2024–2025."

8. National Literacy Institute, "Literacy Statistics 2022–2023."

9. National Literacy Institute, "Literacy Statistics 2022–2023."

10. National Literacy Institute, "Literacy Statistics 2022–2023."

11. Schaffer, "U.S. Public, Private and Charter Schools."

12. Silver, "Top 25 Economies."

Canal is in, and after revealing that she did a report on the Panama Canal in school, she said she thinks it is in Mexico.[13]

In general, children and young adults are completely unaware of the classic literature that has influenced generations and shaped many great minds. Few among them have read or even know the names of St. Augustine, Homer, or Dante. There is minimal understanding of the impact and influence of various forms of government throughout history, or even the meanings of commonly used words in their own language, such as "fascist" and "democracy." Today's children struggle to engage in logical argumentation, relying instead on their emotions as a guide. The individual with the strongest, most visceral feeling often wins the argument, not necessarily because they are correct, but because they are the most passionate.

If you are still thinking, "I'm just not convinced. I still think a modern education can be successful," then I would ask you: why would you choose it? If you have before you two systems, one which has failed at least six generations now and one that has withstood the test of time (over two thousand years), producing many of the greatest minds that Western civilization has ever known—thoughtful, inquisitive, intelligent, impactful minds—why wouldn't you throw the dice on that end? Why not, if it's all the same to you, place your bet on that side of the playing field rather than the other? It's the better wager, if nothing else!

As mentioned, many of the great minds of Western civilization received a classical education in one form or another. The founders of our great nation were classically educated, including Thomas Jefferson, John Adams, James Madison, George Washington, and Alexander Hamilton. Looking back in history, we see Archimedes (who lived in the mid-200s BC), who designed a device for raising water that is still used today, as well as the first odometer, among other things. There's Copernicus, who discovered that planets revolve around the sun and that the earth turns on its axis. We think of men like Galileo Galilei, an influential astronomer, physicist, and engineer, who also received a classical education. Furthermore, Johannes Kepler, who determined how pictures are formed by the eye and discovered that planets move in elliptical orbits around the sun, as well as formulated the three laws of planetary motion still used today to design and launch spaceships, was classically educated. Isaac Newton, who discovered the law of gravity and formulated Newton's laws of motion, also received a classical education. Others like Shakespeare, Leonardo da Vinci, Albert

13. Loveliveserve, "Asking College Students Basic Questions."

Einstein, Frederick Douglass, Oscar Wilde, Martin Luther, C. S. Lewis, J. R. R. Tolkien, St. Benedict, Thomas More, Sigmund Freud, Julius Caesar, St. Augustine, St. Jerome, and St. Ambrose—all these individuals were classically educated. This is only the tip of the iceberg. Movers and shakers in the world have often had this type of education.

What did a classical education uniquely provide to these and many other influential people in history? It equipped them with the tools of learning that they could apply throughout their lives. The reason these individuals had significant influence and impact during their time is that they learned *how to learn*. They also acquired valuable knowledge from many great thinkers before them, which they then built upon to create new ideas and inspire those around them. How did they acquire this knowledge? Firstly, they were very well read. A classical education emphasizes reading Great Books, providing people with a broad view of human history and human experience, along with a vast array of interconnected knowledge that spans the ages. A strong emphasis is additionally placed on critical thinking skills, logic, and rhetoric, which is evidenced throughout each of these men's lives.

A classical education taught these individuals how to teach themselves. I believe the most striking link among people who are classically educated is their lifelong thirst for knowledge and creativity. This was as true in the past as it is today.

A classical education has traditionally included Latin in the curriculum, which could even be considered a hallmark of such an education. This may lead some parents to feel incapable of homeschooling if they wish to provide their children with a classical education. They might think that only a Latin professor at a school can teach their children Latin, especially since few of us have ever studied it. Newly classically minded homeschool families can quickly become enticed by the idea of starting with Spanish or French instead, believing that they are better equipped to teach a language with which they are more familiar.

All of this makes sense. However, let me explain why Latin has been a central part of a classical education for over two thousand years and why you can (and should) teach it if you choose to homeschool.

- Latin forms the basis of all the Romance languages (e.g. Spanish, French, Italian). Learning Latin will make learning any other Romance language far easier.

- Many important historical documents were written in Latin; therefore, knowledge of Latin enables one to read this material in the original language, which provides a better understanding of the author's intentions, style, and tone.

- Latin has a unique way of teaching your brain how to think in terms of precision, patterns, and hypotheses. In Latin, it is typical to be unable to understand a word without referring to all the other words in the sentence, which trains the brain to see connections between things. These skills (precision, recognizing patterns, forming hypotheses, seeing the bigger picture) are highly valuable and easily transferable to other areas of life.

- About half of English (the more complex half) derives from Latin; therefore, knowledge of Latin helps your vocabulary and English comprehension, expanding your ability to communicate.

- Learning English grammar will be much easier and make much more sense if you first learn Latin. Latin is the most consistent, logical, and systematic language in existence, and learning grammatical structure within such a system is more comprehensible for students.

- Latin also forms the root words for much of the vocabulary used in science, medicine, theology, government, philosophy, literature of Western civilization, and the legal field.[14] Knowledge of Latin allows you to more easily access and understand these important fields of study.

Latin is far superior to other Romance languages like Spanish or French as an initial second language choice. And let me encourage you: you can do it. Many programs are available to assist you. Take it one step at a time. A great starting point, if you are unsure how to begin, is to simply get a beginner Latin book for your young student and guide them through the initial lessons. Some books include DVDs, or you can find lessons available for streaming online. Some curricula even offer "live courses" where a teacher lectures in real time while the student listens. You can explore all these options as your child advances in Latin; however, since the initial stages are very basic and easy, you will have no trouble following along and using the teacher's manual for any added assistance. As discussed before, the concern with screens is about their content and the flashing images that

14. Sayers wrote that "Even a rudimentary knowledge of Latin cuts down the labor and pains of learning almost any other subject by at least fifty percent." *Lost Tools*, 23.

can rewire the brain. Older children participating in Latin lecture courses online do not pose the same issues in either of these areas.

In our family, I began teaching Latin while it was still easy, and then when it became more difficult, I contacted the classics department at my alma mater. I asked if there was a doctoral student interested in teaching my kids Latin via FaceTime (for a fee of my choosing). I received a quick response from a student: yes, she did want that job. She has been teaching my children Latin ever since. She is now a teacher at a university, and we FaceTime her once a week. Latin is a subject where you feel like you're killing two birds with one stone because you have to teach grammar to teach Latin. Not being a grammar aficionado, I find this very appealing. It's a great deal. My point is, there are countless ways to teach your child Latin without being a genius yourself (or without losing your mind or going broke). I recommend just starting on the path of a classical education and leaving the rest to God. God has this figured out, and He doesn't want or need you to worry about how He will provide in every way for you and your kids.[15]

15. "Do not worry about your life" (Matt 6:25), and "be anxious for nothing, but in everything by prayer and supplication, with thanksgiving, let your requests be made known to God" (Phil 4:6), as well as "do not fret, it leads *only* to evil" (Ps 37:8; emphasis added).

13

How We Broke Education to Fix It

THE BIG QUESTION NOW is: Why don't we provide this type of education in the United States anymore? When did this modern educational philosophy creep in and take over? In America, the decline started around the time of the Civil War. By the mid-1900s, every tenet of classical educational philosophy had fundamentally vanished. How did this happen? It is a complicated and challenging question to answer, and many books explain it more thoroughly than I can here. This book is only meant to serve as an overview and introduction to this discussion. However, the general summary is that there was a shift in the view of education from one where a child must strive after wisdom and virtue to a focus on training children in patriotism and citizenship. Slowly, aspects of a classical educational system began to be replaced by fundamentally differing ideas about education.

Horace Mann, the Father of Modern American Public Schools, began to gain influence around the 1830s, during the Industrial Revolution.[1] There was a powerful reflection of the factory model in Mann's view of education.[2] Children were sectionalized and compartmentalized into groups solely based on age, and they no longer advanced in their education according to

1. Buck, "Horace Mann's Solution."
2. Kreide, "Literacy Achievement," 4.

mental ability and comprehension of the material. The educational model resembled how a car moves down an assembly line. The industrialists of the time strongly supported the systematization of education to benefit future factory owners. Factories required people who could follow directions and perform repetitive, assigned tasks. The educational system was designed to produce children who would fit the bill. In fact, wealthy Boston industrialist Edmund Dwight believed it was so crucial for factory owners that this new type of education existed that he personally supplied funding for the newly established Massachusetts State Board of Education.[3] A utilitarian view was emerging regarding the purpose of education, fundamentally believing that education should create useful citizens in society.

John Dewey, considered the Father of Progressive Education in America, is one of the men who significantly influenced the transformation of American education in the mid-to-late 1800s. Dewey's foundational viewpoint, which shaped all his educational beliefs, was his rejection of the concept of the sinful nature. This is very important as it underlies his educational philosophies. He was also an atheist and a humanist. He advocated for a democratic process in education where children participated in decision-making regarding their learning. Dewey argued that rather than teaching children truths about the outside world, we should focus on shaping them directly through their experiences. He wrote, "By various agencies, unintentional and designed, a society transforms uninitiated and seemingly alien beings into robust trustees of its own resources and ideals."[4] He goes on to explain how crucial it is to mold these "seemingly alien beings" (i.e., children) into individuals with the tendencies, beliefs, and behaviors that society wishes them to adopt. He did not see this formation as the responsibility of the family. He explicitly stated that this is accomplished through social pressure and the child's desire to "win the approval of others." He recognized and advocated for socialization as a way to strengthen some beliefs and weaken others within a child.[5] The idea that socialization is a vital aspect of education took root and began to grow rapidly, like an invasive plant. This notion would soon entangle nearly all elementary and

3. Ladson-Billings, "From the Achievement Gap," 3–12.

4. Dewey, *Democracy and Education*, 14.

5. Dewey writes about socialization that "it leads him [the child] to have certain plans in order that he may act successfully with others; it strengthens some beliefs and weakens others as a condition of winning the approval of others. Thus, it gradually produces in him a certain system of behavior, a certain disposition of action." Dewey, *Democracy and Education*, 15.

secondary institutions, spreading even into homeschooling, so that many homeschoolers today equate education with socialization, completely misunderstanding the purpose of an education altogether.

Dewey wanted to use education on children, like a surgeon using a scalpel, to shape children into beings who would do the work of society. He emphasized this by saying that "education is the fundamental method of social progress and reform." For Dewey, the value of education was in its ability to reform society. Education was a tool of manipulation, in other words, for societal transformation. For Dewey, education was centered around what is practical and useful. He did not hold the educational practices of previous centuries in high regard. The line "If we teach today's students as we taught yesterday's, we rob them of tomorrow" is often attributed to Dewey; although it is questioned whether he actually said it, he would almost certainly have agreed with it.

He believed that a new way of teaching children was necessary because we have new goals for them. These goals are quite different from being well rounded in historical knowledge, ancient languages, objective truth, and the ability to think and argue. Instead, these goals related to what society needed in its workers. We do not need workers who can think for themselves and argue a point. We do not need workers who can read well and understand ancient historical documents. We need but a few inventors and creative types and many, many more worker bees. He believed in hands-on activities and building on the prior interests of children through active learning. He wrote, "There is no such thing as genuine knowledge and fruitful understanding except as the offspring of doing."[6] In almost every way, this was a massive shift from classical education, historically speaking. Of course, that was viewed as only a positive advancement.

It was through these and other influential men in the 1800s and 1900s that an entirely different fundamental viewpoint about education developed, shifting it dramatically from being an individual's pursuit of knowledge and virtue to a focus on creating useful people who can practically serve society in an age of industry. God was no longer a foundational aspect of education either. Indeed, during this period of the nineteenth century, the famous German philosopher Friedrich Nietzsche famously wrote that "God is dead."[7] We can see how that viewpoint crept into and completely took over educational philosophy. We lost the concept of

6. Dewey, *Democracy and Education*, 283.
7. Nietzsche, *Joyful Wisdom*, 275.

sinfulness within ourselves and our children, which by nature demands entirely different approaches and responses. In its place, we inserted the view that there is no sin and no God. Therefore, we ourselves became the arbiter of the truth. The truth, generally speaking, is now subjective. If you don't have a higher moral power—a God—saying what's right and wrong and what you should do, then who's to say what's right and wrong? Who's to say if something is true or not true?

Curricula both within the government and in the homeschool arena have had no problem placing themselves as the arbiters for truth and deciding what children should and shouldn't learn according to their own subjective value systems. Over time, we can see how all of this easily morphed into a focus on how our education makes us feel. That's not a far leap if you think about it. That's because when you lose sight of seeking the truth—when you lose sight of gaining wisdom for the sake of gaining wisdom—what is left for education to be about? If education isn't about objective truth, it must be about subjective truth. And subjective truth means we are all our own standards for things. How we feel is then the highest good, because it's all about us, our emotions, and our experiences. What we believe is up to us, and we have no ultimate purpose. We just want to feel good and get the right answer, check the box, and move on. And a modern education feeds into that. Just do the work, regurgitate what I want you to say, get your stamp of approval, and move on in life.

The classical model has you looking outside of yourself at what is greater, good, and true out in the world and in the universe. The classical model has you reading the prominent figures in history and the giants of literature to better understand reality and to build on ideas and constructs of others' hard work and imagination. A classical education does not stick its nose up at the past but embraces it with interest and fascination. A classical education is a constant search for objective knowledge. It changes the trajectory of our focus from being on what is inside of ourselves to what is outside of ourselves as we search for wisdom and find beauty in past discoveries and others' ideas, as well as our own. That is why there isn't a curriculum in modern education that connects the dots of history to science to theology to astronomy to math. Subjects do not connect in modern education, and knowledge doesn't interlock within a designed and cogent universe. Instead, they are independent, sterile, and autonomous subjects. They are subjects unto themselves that are there only as a material, disposable means to an end.

Let's stop right here and highlight another important fundamental difference between classical education and modern education: the view each takes of children's abilities. A classical approach believes in the ability of children in general and the incredible potential of each child in particular to learn. Historically, a child in the Middle Ages would have completed the Trivium by around fourteen years old,[8] ending his studies by composing

> a thesis upon some theme set by his masters or chosen by himself, and afterwards [he was expected] to defend his thesis against the criticism of the faculty. By this time, he would have learned, or woe betide him, not merely to write well, but to speak audibly and intelligibly from a platform, and to use his wits quickly when heckled. There would be questions, cogent and shrewd, from those who had already run the gauntlet of debate.[9]

Compare this with modern education, which believes in a concept of "no child left behind" or "every student succeeds," encouraging only the bare minimum standards to be met, rather than exceeded. This way, every child can continue along the assembly line of grades until they reach completion by turning a certain age, at which point they graduate. This is considered educational success. They have become robotic enough to meet society's material needs. Children progress regardless of their capacity for critical thinking or what they have learned or achieved. Expectations are purposely low instead of purposely high, so that everyone can continue down the assembly line.

Exceeding standards causes a problem within this system. It throws everything off. A child of seven, for example, could never be allowed to do the work of a child of ten years old, not only because it would cause a disaster in the production line but also because that child has already been deemed *incapable* of doing that work. You could never even attempt such a thing! It would be bad for the child because we have presupposed that

8. I have occasionally heard a strange argument from some when historical expectations for children are discussed. The argument goes along these lines: people used to live much shorter lives in past times, therefore they did extraordinary things at young ages. They didn't have as much time to wait. But this makes little sense. A person still had, for example, only fourteen years of life on this earth and yet they were somehow managing to argue cogently and coherently in a public forum. The fact people tended to die younger does not account for abilities, learning, or intelligence. Their life span did not, in other words, endow them with special magic powers that cannot be conjured up today. What is demonstrated by historical examples of this nature is that children can rise to meet expectations and are in fact, capable of a great many things.

9. Sayers, *Lost Tools*, 14–15.

children cannot do it. It is like Thomas Jefferson's rejection of miracles on the basis of an *a priori* assumption that miracles are impossible. It is circular reasoning: something is impossible because I say it is impossible, and if I say it is impossible, it must be impossible. A similar thing has occurred here. Children are viewed as unable to conquer difficult things, so they are not given difficult things to conquer.

We have greatly underestimated children's capabilities, and in so doing, we have diluted their education. The end result is that children's capabilities are distilled to their lowest common denominators, combined into a container with all sorts of modern assumptions, and boiled until they've lost all individuality, passion, and pursuit of excellence, ending up being siphoned into a container labeled "for society."

We should not doubt that this view of children has seeped into every nook and cranny of the discussion surrounding them, including the topic of discipline in the classroom. Society says we should not expect young children to behave, and as children are called such until eighteen years old, we often end up wondering why there isn't a sudden behavioral light switch that goes off when they enter college. We shouldn't wonder that we have a bunch of childish adults! We have held them to an almost nonexistent standard their entire lives and treated them as other than what they are: intelligent, capable, enthusiastic, and yet also sinful little human beings.

In the end, modern education has a foundation in an entirely different premise—one that holds to little objective truth. Truth is fungible and individual today. It's based on experiences, and therefore it isn't universal. Children are taught each subject as though it's entirely independent from other subjects, and the result is inevitably joylessness. If there is any interest ever seen by a child about a subject, it often comes from a hands-on activity they find momentarily interesting and gain little from. It is assumed that they should physically do things as much as possible because they cannot *truly* learn otherwise. Having been the subject of many hands-on activities, and watched many others taking place, I can safely say I have yet to see one involving any of the core subjects apart from the more advanced sciences and a few math concepts wherein I would say the hands-on nature of the activity added anything of merit to the learning process that was worth the time expended on it. Most of the time, nothing new was learned at all, and even when something small was gained, it never equaled in worth the amount of time spent in doing it.

I remember a leaf project in high school, which is a perfect example of this, and I could list many others. We were tasked with collecting leaves from various types of trees, putting them in a binder, and labeling them. I do not recall how many leaves we had to collect, but it was a substantial number. This project consumed an exorbitant amount of time and took several days to complete. I learned absolutely nothing about trees and retained not a single fact about them.

Let's consider applying this to another aspect of life. Imagine you are preparing dinner for your family and you spend a total of six hours cooking in the kitchen. The result? A meal that feeds one of your three children, and only half of their needed portion at that. Would you consider that time well spent? Or would you prefer, if you had to spend six hours cooking, to prepare a hearty meal that could feed your entire family and last for three days? I know for sure which option I would choose! Education is not entirely dissimilar. We have only so many hours each day to fill our children's heads with good things. They have only so much focus time, and we would do well to use it wisely rather than finding many and various hands-on activities for them that simply serve to suck up their time and add little value to their overall learning. It is unnecessary to throw the baby out with the bathwater here and disregard any hands-on learning, but the extreme emphasis modern education places on this is misplaced and hinders children's learning.

One reason people might assume that children who sit and listen to a teacher are not genuinely learning is that they appear to be passive.[10] We cannot see inside a child's brain when they are working and learning, and since we cannot observe what is happening in there, it may raise questions about whether learning is actually taking place. When a child is engaged in a hands-on activity, we can see them doing it, which assures us that activity is occurring. It feels productive to us. This perspective is rather materialistic and, interestingly, somewhat one-dimensional.

Children have a very lively and active inner life that is not entirely dissimilar to adults. They have many thoughts and contemplate various ideas. Children learning from an intelligent and communicative teacher will naturally be quieter than usual as they process new and exciting information. Their minds will be busy making all sorts of connections. Silence, contrary to modern societal belief, is not always a negative thing;

10. It is also hard for children whose brains are used to flashing images and constant entertainment to focus these days, since their brains have been rewired.

it is necessary for processing material beyond surface level. It doesn't have to mean guaranteed boredom.

A key to ensuring engagement and learning lies in the content being taught, not in the theatrics and showmanship of the activities. What I mean is that if you spend a week teaching about salmon, a child will surely be bored and need activities to keep them engaged. However, if you spend a week teaching about a wide variety of ocean life found within a particular ecosystem, what an ecosystem even is and how the various life forms interact with each other, what feeds on what, why they thrive in that area, the ocean depth wherein the various life forms are found, the water temperature that supports their existence and how everything varies between other bodies of water, you will find a fascinated group of learners who are interacting with the material in a way that is just as active as their "hands-on" counterparts but who are learning a great deal more.

We need to understand that a classical education is a rigorous education. In American education, the term "rigorous" is almost like a bad word, isn't it? It kind of makes us shift uncomfortably in our seats. It's not something you hear in your local homeschool co-op. It's not written about. It's not often in curriculum descriptions either. No one would promote a homeschool program by calling it *rigorous*! Heavens. You might as well advertise your curriculum with the term "child abuse!"

But please don't make the mistake of misunderstanding what a rigorous education means for your child. Don't let that word magic scare you. It is not, in fact, a bad word. It's a word that carries many blessings for your child. A rigorous education is simply one that offers a comprehensive approach, which, by its nature, includes mastering complex concepts, actively engaging firsthand with written and historical material, using analytical skills, and employing logic. It is essentially an education where a child must exert themselves to learn, as has historically been expected. Children will rise to meet expectations under these circumstances.

This is an education that encourages a child to reach their full potential. That's all it is. It is a gift to your child and to their future because it helps to tear down roadblocks. When we do not ensure our children receive a rigorous education, we are, in a way, handicapping them. We are not equipping them with the necessary tools, both in self-control and in knowledge, to achieve what they aspire to accomplish. They can overcome this, but it will be much harder for them than it would have been otherwise. Remember, children are designed to thrive on learning, and they are happiest when they discover new things and are taught to control their sinful nature. Therefore, both in the short- and long-term, a challenging education is the best option.

A truly classical education will always challenge students because of the way it is structured. There are many new things to learn—an endless amount of beauty and knowledge to take in. It is structured to teach students how to work hard at learning something, and the reward is understanding the world around them, understanding history, seeing how things connect and influence one another, and understanding literature. Students develop competency, confidence, and self-esteem because they are gaining in wisdom and virtue. However, it's a process that requires work.

Many programs today, and modern education in general, want kids to "take the lead" and insist that education should be something they want to do, or you're doing it wrong. But that is a dangerous mindset. It is not good to teach children that they should only pursue things they want to do and find exciting. It isn't good to instill the belief that every task comes with an immediate reward. Sometimes, effort is necessary to achieve a worthwhile outcome, and sometimes you don't receive immediate gratification. Sometimes you have to wait. Can you imagine what kind of adult they will become if they don't learn this during their formative years?

You probably don't need to imagine; you likely know an adult or two who expects a reward for everything they do and feels incredibly entitled. They act as though the world revolves around them and become upset when required to do something they don't want to do. Their primary goal is their pleasure. They pursue it like it is their full-time job, and a common trait among these adults is their inward focus. Lacking self-discipline, they are easily distracted by their immediate impulses and desires.

While a classical education is not a complete solution to this problem, high expectations from this type of program can foster an outward turning in children. They are gently steered away from prioritizing short-term gratification in their education, so that their studies and quest for knowledge are not contingent on whether they feel inclined to do the work at any given moment. Self-discipline can be developed through a challenging and stimulating educational program that continually raises the bar for student achievement.

If you are wondering if there are limits for a child if they are classically trained versus trained within a modern system, let me tell you an interesting story. In Germany in the nineteenth century, there were two distinct educational paths. There was the classical path, which led students to university, and another path dedicated to science, technology, math, and modern languages, which led to the "Realschule," also known as a technical school, and subsequently into a professional school or a job in the industry.[11]

One might assume that the advancements in quantum mechanics and physics would have been made by those who received the technical schooling. After all, they are the ones in the trenches, working with the things that people in school only theorize about, right? That's true, but the results were not that way. The developments and discoveries made in these technical areas were almost across the board *solely* from people who received a classical education. This presents a fascinating control study that is hard to find anywhere else in the world: two groups existing side by side in the same country, receiving two entirely different types of education simultaneously. It supports the fact that providing your child with a classical education does not limit them in any way. You are not preventing them from understanding modern concepts or from working in a modern world. In fact, you are doing the opposite and equipping them to make a difference.

Today, education has unfortunately become centered around grades and tests instead of on achieving knowledge and truth. The primary reward a child experiences in school usually comes from their grades. That's the end goal. They aren't rewarded with the natural joy that arises from learning fascinating facts about the universe and connecting prior knowledge to those facts. They aren't praised for thinking critically or engaging in argument. Instead, they are only allowed to create within boxes and are punished when they stray outside the box. They search for some kind of meaning and find it's solely about the grades. That's all there is, so that's all education means to them. We do not want this to happen to our children.

11. Kopff, "Greek to Us."

14

The Consuming Fire
Known as Fear

THERE ARE SO MANY things for parents to fear in the world today, aren't there? In addition to our children's health and physical safety, parents confront a multitude of worries regarding their children's future. What kind of world will it be when our children become adults? How will we afford college? What if they struggle to find a job? Parents considering homeschooling face many additional concerns. A list of common worries can be found below:

I'm worried my kid won't be "socialized."

I'm worried I am not smart enough to teach them.

I'm worried my kid won't like being homeschooled.

I'm worried it'll be too expensive.

I'm worried my kid will be weird.

I'm worried about what my family will think.

I'm worried about what I'll do when the subjects are advanced.

I'm worried I am not organized or self-disciplined enough.

I'm worried I can't get my kid to do their work.

I'm worried about finding the right curriculum or choosing the wrong one.

I'm worried I won't have the patience.

I'm worried about being around my kids 24/7.

I'm worried I can't homeschool and keep house.

What do you notice about all of these sentences? They all begin with "I'm worried." I understand that. Worry and I are old enemies. We face each other in battle often. Whenever I start to fear things, I try to remember to turn to God's Word to see what He says about this battle. "Do not fret, it leads only to evil."[1] This is one of my favorite verses because it reminds me that fear literally cannot lead anywhere good. Even if I have every good reason to worry, God tells me it leads *only* to evil and cannot lead anywhere else. Therefore, I know that nothing but evil will come from giving in to fear and making my decisions based on it. We only have the facts of today, and we should base our decisions on those facts. The future is where fear comes in since we don't know or control it. God has willed us to be in this position. We have to trust Him that He will work "all things . . . together for good for those who love God and have been called according to His purpose."[2]

A few of my favorite verses to bring with me into battle are:

Philippians 4:19
And my God will meet *all your needs* according to the riches of his glory in Christ Jesus (emphasis added).

Matthew 6:31–33
So do not worry, saying, "What shall we eat?" or "What shall we drink?" or "What shall we wear?" For the pagans run after all these things, and your heavenly Father knows that you need them. But seek first his kingdom and his righteousness, and all these things will be given to you as well.

Exodus 14:13–14:
You only need to remain calm; the Lord will fight for you.

1. Ps 37:8.
2. Rom 8:28.

Deuteronomy 1:30–31

The Lord our God will lead the way. He will fight on our side, just as he did when we saw him do all those things to the Egyptians. And you know that the Lord has taken care of us the whole time we've been in the desert, just as you might carry one of your children.

One of the primary fears for many parents is that their child will not be socialized if they homeschool. Ask a parent why they send their kids to school, and the majority will answer, "For socialization."[3] Many moms and dads are terrified that if they homeschool, their child will not be "socialized." I explained in the previous chapter where this idea of socialization originated and how it is used within the educational system to instill beliefs and ideologies into children through social pressure. When children are pressed into molds in this fashion, they become much easier to control because they are taught to think similarly rather than critically. When making a decision about this issue of socialization, we need to examine the facts concerning it so that we can choose a path based on reality rather than a vague fear used by the devil to create a fictional reality.

First, to talk about socialization, we need to understand what it actually is. According to the dictionary, socialization is "the process by which somebody, especially a child, learns to behave in a way that is acceptable in their society."[4] Many parents mistakenly use the word "socialization" to mean "having friends," leading them to believe that their child must undergo the process of socialization to have friends.

To clarify, socialization is *not* merely the act of having friends. These terms are not synonymous. Socialization serves as a tool—a process—which is intended to make children behave well and treat one another kindly while teaching them how to act appropriately in society. Appropriately in society . . . right behavior . . . hmmm. You may be asking yourself, "Where are all these socialized kids who act appropriately and treat each other kindly? Where are they hiding?" Because the last time you checked, the kids you see around do not seem to fit that description.

If that's what you're thinking, you're absolutely right. They don't fit the description of well-behaved, polite, kind people, even though most kids have been properly socialized. The reason is that parents have latched

3. I have never heard anyone say that they are sending their child to public school "for the excellent education," even if they are sending their children to private school. This is very strange, seeing as school is, at least theoretically, supposed to be about an education.

4. Oxford Learner's Dictionaries, "Socialization."

on to this word "socialization" in hopes that it will do their job for them. Little Suzy talks back to her mom, so her mom figures school is the answer! Little Suzy will learn not to talk back and will listen to authority because she will be pressured into doing so. Then there's little Debbie, who won't do schoolwork for her mom, but her mom is *sure* she'll do work for a teacher, so off little Debbie goes to school.

Little Johnny throws tantrums and hits other kids when mom is around, and she just doesn't know what to do with him! Boys will be boys, you know! But even with that slogan on repeat, Mom reaches her breaking point. The solution? Send little Johnny to school! His classmates will teach him that these behaviors aren't socially acceptable, and he'll change and come home a nice, new boy.

The problem is that this isn't what happens at all. The parent is merely postponing the necessary task of correcting their child's stubborn heart and sinful inclinations. They are avoiding the difficulty of addressing sin, which means that the sin will grow, leading to an even bigger problem in the future that they will not be able to ignore. It is better, then, regardless of the educational setting you choose, to confront discipline problems head-on, the moment you notice them. This is our God-given responsibility as parents, and choosing any other path will inevitably result in disaster.

When parents send their children into a group of peers with the express intention of miraculously transforming bad behaviors into good, it's unsurprising that *none* of the children learn how to behave. Instead, it resembles a real-life, modern-day *Lord of the Flies*, where the children essentially eat each other alive. The reason children cannot and do not teach each other appropriate behavior is simply that water doesn't rise above its own level. This means that children can't instruct one another on right and good behavior because they themselves are still in the process of learning what constitutes appropriate behavior. That's why they need their parents to be present, teaching them how to interact well with others.

When considering socialization, we should also remember what it was like for us as children when we faced pressure, compared to how it is now that we are adults. As adults, we are far less influenced by our environment than children are (although we can be highly influenced under the right circumstances!). For those of us who can't remember that far back, studies exist to illustrate this. One such paper separated children into groups based on age: children (8–11 years), young adolescents (12–14 years), mid-adolescents (15–18 years), young adults (19–25 years), and adults (26–59 years). The study showed that the three youngest age groups were the most susceptible to "prosocial influences," meaning they were easily manipulated to change their verbal desires and answers based on what the child perceived to be the majority opinion. This same paper cites a number of other studies that have demonstrated the incredible malleability and susceptibility of children to social pressure. The younger they are, the more easily they are influenced. By the time they reach young adulthood (over 19), they are far less likely to change their opinion on things based on pressure.[5]

We see this manifest in various overt ways, such as the significant issue of sexual orientation and trans ideology. A new Gallup poll showed that "overall, each younger generation is about twice as likely as the generation that preceded it to identify as LGBTQ+."[6] We also see that 5–20 percent of sixth graders and 14–42 percent of eighth graders now engage in sexual intercourse, and a "concerning percentage" of students engage in other "sexual risk behaviors."[7] Children are indeed being influenced, but the results are clearly not favorable to us following suit!

What do we say to the parents who don't care about right behaviors and healthy friendships? They just don't want their child to turn out "weird." They want their child to fit in with everyone else. We've all met people like this. They are very sure that adequate socialization leads to happy children who have many friends. This reveals something very important about their belief system that they may not even realize: happiness and friendship come from the world. Friendship is not a gift from God; it is something you can create by yourself, for yourself. Friendship is inherently good, a concept that ignores the reality and nature of bad friendships. There exists a rather insidious view that the highest good is to have lots and lots of friends. We need only look at current or past pop stars with all their broken relationships, multiple marriages, drug and alcohol addictions, and mental health issues to recognize that friendship, popularity, and worldly acceptance do not produce happiness. We desire godly, true friends for our kids, not just a group of influential peers leading them astray!

What socialization itself requires for acceptance and fitting in is conformity. Conformity is not a net positive. James writes, "Don't you know that friendship with the world means enmity against God?"[8] When we direct our children's education toward a focus on friendship with the world,

5. Foulkes et al., "Age Differences," 1–9.
6. Jones, "LGBTQ+ Identification."
7. Moore et al., "Sexual Behaviors," 1.
8. Jas 4:4.

we are guaranteeing that their eyes are fixed on the wrong things. Being different from the world is not a problem; rather, it is the result of being a Christian. We don't blend in and aren't going to blend in, and we shouldn't want to. We should stand confidently in the world while not being of the world. Jesus prayed on earth to God the Father, saying, "I have given them your word and the world has hated them, for they are not of the world any more than I am of the world. My prayer is not that you take them out of the world but that you protect them from the evil one."[9] Hatred from the world is what you're guaranteed as a Christian. This is not what we parents want to hear. We want to hear that our children can feel love from others and have friendships that strengthen and support them . . . *and they can.* The question isn't if they can have that. The question is *how you can achieve that.* This is a good and natural desire, to want friendships for your children, and God will provide those friendships. He will do it. We can rest in simply listening to what God says and remembering that we have been "called out" of this world.[10] We are different. Instead of pointing our children towards social acceptance as the primary good and verbalizing a fixation on it, we should point them towards praying for good friendships and waiting patiently on the Lord to provide.

It's crucial to remember that just as God gave you the right spouse out of the millions of people in the world, so He will also provide you and your children with the right friends. When we trust God in this way, we release a burden that we are not meant to carry. It may not be in our timing, but it will be in His perfect timing. He hasn't forgotten our needs, and He won't ever forget them. Sometimes He asks us to wait, and at other times, He provides immediately. We know that no matter what He has planned for us, it will be for our good,[11] and it will turn out better than we could have asked or imagined.[12] He will provide all things, including friendships.

My husband was in the military for several years, and we moved frequently. With each move, there were initially times of extreme loneliness. During those times when I was waiting for His provision of local friends for our family, I turned to Lam 3:25–29: "The Lord is good to those whose hope is in him, to the one who seeks him; it is good to wait quietly for the salvation of the Lord. It is good for a man to bear the yoke while he is young. Let him sit alone in silence, for the Lord has laid it on

9. John 17:15–16.

10. The Greek word for church is "ekklesia" which means "called out."

11. Rom 8:28.

12. Eph 3:20.

him. Let him bury his face in the dust—there may yet be hope." If you or your children are experiencing silence, it is good, according to God. It may not feel good while you are in it; it feels painful. However, God, whose ways are not our ways and whose thoughts are not our thoughts, says it is for our good.[13] The Lord has laid this on us for a reason, and He will bring something beautiful out of that experience.

One thing I noticed early on during those periods of loneliness was that it brought me closer to the Lord and helped me connect more deeply with my children. It also had an unexpected effect on the kids, who grew much closer to one another during these times and formed profound bonds with their siblings—something they will cherish for the rest of their lives. We also discovered that friendship can arise from the most unexpected places. Intergenerational friendships blossomed throughout the various churches we attended and the neighborhoods we lived in. Sometimes my prayer for friendship has taken the form of a grandparent figure, a teacher (like our neighbor who teaches the kids woodcarving), a role model, or a child of a completely different age. Just as the church of Christ is intergenerational, it is good and right for our children to experience diverse relationships and friendships—whatever the Lord has prepared for them. As we continue to pray for the right friends who will positively influence our children during their most formative years, we can encourage one another as parents to focus on the work God has given us to do: to raise children who are strong in their faith and engaged in good works.

Instead of viewing socialization as the solution to our parenting problems and concerns, and trying to mold our children to be like other children, we can celebrate our children's differences. Our goal is not for them to appear just like everyone else. We want to strengthen them in their individuality precisely because they are members of the body of Christ, where each member has a distinct role to fulfill.

As parents, we encounter numerous decisions, and we strive to approach each one with complete confidence in the Lord's good purpose for our lives. We can view friendship and all our parenting choices through the lens of God's Word, with absolute trust in Him, instead of viewing them through the lens of fear regarding future "what ifs." We have nothing to fear. God is faithful, and He will direct our paths.[14]

---

13. Isa 55:8

14. "In all your ways acknowledge him, and he will make your paths straight." Prov 3:6

15

Continuing in Our Vocation as Parents

IT IS EASY TO get lost in a sea of good ideas and well-meaning advice. It's simple to wander from the path we started on or to become distracted by all the new, glittering, and enticing things we encounter along the way. As Christian parents, we want to stay laser-focused on what is *most important* for our child's formation, and we want to measure everything we do and every decision we make against God's Word and reality (i.e., the facts of this world). Remember, God is the God of truth, so facts are on His side. We do well, therefore, when we seek the truth (or reality) in all things. We have nothing to fear by doing so, and we will find that it only reinforces the path God has outlined in Scripture.

When we encounter an issue with our child and feel uncertain about how to handle it, we should first consider what God has said about the matter. Does He address it? I'm willing to bet He does in most cases, at least on a fundamental level, when we think about the essence of the problem. As we seek specific parenting advice or ideas, we need to evaluate how what we hear aligns with God's Word. To do this, we must first know His Word and be familiar with what He teaches. Then, if anything contradicts it, even in the smallest way, that part of the advice must be discarded.

When discussing our child's education, it is true that God has not directly spoken about this specific topic, nor has He addressed the issue of education when you boil it down to its fundamental questions of style and type. Therefore, we should examine outside objective evidence (from studies and statistics) and combine those facts with what we can observe in the outside world, using that information to make wise decisions about the type of education we want to provide for our child. Read the studies and the news. Look at the kids around you in church or at school and ask them questions. Observe the current situation with your eyes. Remember, we are not asking what we *wish* the situation to be, or what we *think* a modern education should produce. We are not creating an alternate reality in our minds. We are simply looking at the actual state of things and making decisions accordingly.

While we don't have direct information from God about the type of education we should provide for our children, we do know that He does care about what goes into the heart and mind. He does care about formation, and He cares very much about children. We can observe how our choices about education greatly influence children emotionally, mentally, and spiritually. Education is the formation of the brain and of the self. Therefore, our choices about it truly matter. *Education matters.*

We know, as we carefully search for the best route to take, that we must ask ourselves the tough questions. What is the best possible education I can provide for my child? Not, "What is best for me?" Not, "What does my bank account say is best for it?" Not, "What are my friends doing with their kids?" Not, "How will my family fit into a group?" But, "What is best for my child based on the evidence before me?" Then leave the rest to God. You are in His hands, and your child is in His care. He promises to remain faithful to you, and you can take great comfort in that promise.

There are temptations as we walk this road. We don't want to misalign our priorities or lose focus on what we are building, which is a solid framework in early childhood, firmly established on the Word of God. This is easy to do. St. Augustine believed in rightly ordered love,[1] which is to say that virtue and goodness cannot be achieved if our loves are disordered. What are our loves? They are our affections and desires. We must keep God first and order our other affections and desires rightly after that. As Christian parents, this means we put God first, our spouse second, and our

---

1. Augustine, *City of God* 15.22.

children third; all other things must come after these top three priorities and should be ranked according to their eternal value.

This means that whatever is best for our child always takes precedence over what others may want us to do, for example. Our child's safety is more important than social acceptance from other parents. Our child's ability to ferret out the truth in this age of false information overload, well, it seems to me that is a higher good than "socialization," especially in light of our previous discussion on the topic. How you feel comfort-wise then is rightly relegated to a spot very low on the totem pole because so many things are more important than that. Your child's mental, physical, and spiritual wellbeing is far more significant than that, sitting high up there on the pole, and that is exactly where it should be.

Understanding reality and ordering our loves towards that reality, then, is what we aim to achieve. However, to do so, we must know what God says; otherwise, we are acting blindly. His Word is a lamp to our feet, the Bible says, and a light to our path. It cannot illuminate our path without our knowledge of what it says, however. The danger of irregularly reading God's Word is that the path remains unlit. As a result, we may stray onto other routes, following our own desires and our society instead of God, often without even realizing it. We are in great need of God's constant guidance, and for that, we need to remain connected to where that guidance can be found, namely, in His Word.

Even when there are a million distractions vying for our attention, we want to remain focused and "major in the majors" as parents. To achieve this, we must understand our goals, and it helps to be very specific about them. Write them down if that would help you. Create a list with your spouse. Rank those priorities in order of true importance.

My husband and I reflected on this, and we realized that we want our children to grow up in the grace and knowledge of our Lord and Savior,[2] as Peter wrote. That is our main goal and everything we do, therefore, should point back to that. We aim to provide our children with a rigorous education to enrich their knowledge of the truth and foster self-discipline in their hearts. All truth connects back to the one true, living God, so knowledge of the truth in any area of their lives helps equip them to face the onslaught of the world's lies, opinions, teachings, and ideologies. Being well educated also enables our children to connect more easily with people from various backgrounds and on different levels, allowing them

2. 2 Pet 3:18.

to impact many others and potentially lead many to Christ. Receiving a good education prepares our children for whatever God has planned for them, so education has become another high priority.

Knowledge is powerful in all areas of life, especially when it comes to knowledge of God's Word. We want to equip our children to make a difference in this world and to follow the Lord all the days of their lives. Self-discipline, a necessary component of Christianity and inherently present in a rigorous education, when properly paired with God's Word, nurtures virtues in the heart and helps our children combat vices. All our efforts and priorities focus on the fundamental idea that we want to follow Christ.

Throughout early childhood, we encounter a special and unique period of time wherein God provides us with every advantage and tool needed to build a firm foundation in our children's hearts and minds. He has blessed us with children who are impressionable, adaptable, and eager to learn. His Word is there to guide us in the way we should go. He has also given us freedom here in America to raise our children as we wish and even to choose the type of education they will receive. This is a tremendous gift. When we make wise use of this time, placing great value on instilling good things in our child's heart, we fulfill the work God has given us to do.

Early childhood is unlike any other time in life. Children at this stage are loving, malleable, impressionable, trusting, excitable, enthusiastic, smart, and capable young people. They have limitless potential. During early childhood, if we actively engage as parents, we will find ourselves more drained and taxed than at any other stage of our child's development (or, let's be perfectly honest, of our entire lives), because it is during this stage that our children are the most dependent on us and in greatest need of discipline and guidance. It feels constant because it is constant. It can be so tempting sometimes as a parent to give up because it seems like this will never end, and that we're too tired to continue doing the same thing day after day after day. We keep failing anyway, so how could any good come from what we are doing? Take heart. The fruit will appear before you know it. Keep picking up your cross and following the Lord. He doesn't work through perfect. He works through the sinner. He works through *you*. And He has promised He will never leave you or forsake you. When you are weak, you will be able to see His immense strength.[3] So we can

---

3. "But he said to me, 'My grace is sufficient for you, for my power is made perfect in weakness.' Therefore, I will boast all the more gladly about my weaknesses, so that Christ's power may rest on me." 2 Cor 12:9.

confidently make our parenting decisions based on the facts of today and not the fear of tomorrow or the fear of our own weaknesses. In every new moment, in every breath, He will help you in this calling. And when all this is over, which will be in a twinkling of an eye, when the last trumpet sounds, He will say to you because of Christ, "My good and faithful servant." Come, Lord Jesus!

The Good and the Great

Book Checklist for Kids[1]

Level 1

- ☐ Bob Books series[2] (Set 1 & 2)
- ☐ The Dick and Jane Reading Collection[3]
- ☐ Biscuit series[4]
- ☐ *Little Critter: A Green, Green Garden*[5]
- ☐ *Joseph and His Brothers*[6]
- ☐ *Little Critter: Just Helping My Dad*[7]
- ☐ *Noah and the Ark*[8]
- ☐ *Whose Hat Is It?*[9]

---

1. Recommended use for literature class.
2. Bobby Lynn Maslen.
3. Penguin Young Readers.
4. Alyssa Satin Capucilli.
5. Mercer Mayer.
6. ZonderKidz.
7. Mercer Mayer.
8. ZonderKidz.
9. Valeri Gorbachev.

- ☐ *Moses and the King*[10]
- ☐ *Baby Jesus Is Born*[11]
- ☐ *Daniel and the Lions*[12]
- ☐ *The Child's Primer*[13]
- ☐ *Owl at Home*[14]
- ☐ *Mouse Tales*[15]
- ☐ *Clifford series*[16]

Dr. Seuss Beginner Books:

- ☐ *Hop on Pop*
- ☐ *Fred and Ted's Road Trip*
- ☐ *Fred and Ted Go Camping*
- ☐ *Fox in Socks*
- ☐ *Are You My Mother?*
- ☐ *Green Eggs and Ham*
- ☐ *Great Day for Up*
- ☐ *The Ear Book*
- ☐ *I Can Read with My Eyes Shut!*
- ☐ *The Cat in the Hat*
- ☐ *The Cat in the Hat Comes Back*
- ☐ *Mrs. Wow Never Wanted a Cow*
- ☐ *The Foot Book*
- ☐ *The Ear Book*

10. ZonderKidz.
11. ZonderKidz.
12. ZonderKidz.
13. Sidney G. Firman and Ethel H. Maltby.
14. Arnold Lobel.
15. Arnold Lobel.
16. Norman Bridwell.

☐ *The Eye Book*

☐ *The Nose Book*

My First Little House Books:[17]

☐ *The Deer in the Wood*

☐ *A Little Prairie House*

☐ *Prairie Day*

☐ *Summertime in the Big Woods*

☐ *Going West*

☐ *Going to Town*

☐ *Winter on the Farm*

☐ *Dance at Grandpa's*

☐ *Winter Days in the Big Woods*

☐ *County Fair*

☐ *A Little House Birthday*

☐ *Sugar Snow*

☐ *Christmas in the Big Woods*

Level 2

☐ *Caps for Sale*[18]

☐ *Billy and Blaze*[19]

☐ *Blueberries for Sal*[20]

☐ *A Chair for My Mother*[21]

☐ *Corduroy*[22]

17. Laura Ingalls Wilder.
18. Esphyr Slobodkina.
19. C. W. Anderson.
20. Robert McCloskey.
21. Vera B. Williams. A Caldecott Honor book.
22. Don Freeman.

☐ *Curious George*[23]

☐ *Dr. DeSoto*[24]

☐ *Floss*[25]

☐ *Frog & Toad All Year*[26]

☐ *Frog & Toad Are Friends*[27]

☐ *Harry the Dirty Dog*[28]

☐ *Harry by the Sea*[29]

☐ *If You Give a Mouse a Cookie*[30]

☐ *If You Give a Pig a Pancake*[31]

☐ *The Little Engine that Could*[32]

☐ *Amelia Bedelia*[33]

☐ *The Biggest Bear*[34]

☐ *Henry and Mudge*[35]

☐ *Annie and Snowball and the Wintery Freeze*[36]

☐ *Little Bear*[37]

☐ *Madeline*[38]

23. H. A. Rey.
24. William Steig.
25. Kim Lewis.
26. Arnold Lobel.
27. Arnold Lobel. A Caldecott Honor book.
28. Gene Zion.
29. Gene Zion.
30. Laura Numeroff.
31. Laura Numeroff.
32. Watty Piper.
33. Peggy Parish.
34. Lynd Ward. Caldecott Medal.
35. Cynthia Rylant.
36. Cynthia Rylant.
37. Else Holmelund Minarik.
38. Ludwig Bemelmans. A Caldecott Honor book.

- ☐ *Miss Nelson Is Missing*[39]
- ☐ *Mr. Putter and Tabby Pour the Tea*[40]
- ☐ *Nate the Great*[41]
- ☐ *Nate the Great and the Lost List*[42]
- ☐ *A New Coat for Anna*[43]
- ☐ *Stone Soup*[44]
- ☐ *Peter Rabbit*[45]
- ☐ *The Emperor's New Clothes*[46]
- ☐ *Sammy the Seal*[47]
- ☐ *Make Way for Ducklings*[48]
- ☐ *Morris the Moose*[49]
- ☐ *One Morning in Maine*[50]
- ☐ *The Story of Ping*[51]
- ☐ *Wagon Wheels*[52]
- ☐ *Brave Irene*[53]
- ☐ *Little Bear's Friend*[54]

39. Harry G. Allard Jr.
40. Cynthia Rylant and Arthur Howard.
41. Marjorie Weinman Sharmat.
42. Marjorie Weinman Sharmat.
43. Harriet Ziefert.
44. Marcia Brown. A Caldecott Honor book.
45. Beatrix Potter.
46. Hans Christian Anderson. Retold by Ned Bustard.
47. Syd Hoff.
48. Robert McCloskey. A Caldecott Medal book.
49. B. Wiseman.
50. Robert McCloskey. A Caldecott Honor book.
51. Marjorie Flack and Kurt Wiese.
52. Barbara Brenner.
53. William Steig.
54. Else Homelund Minarik.

☐ *Harry and the Lady Next Door*[55]

☐ *No Roses for Harry*[56]

☐ *Danny and the Dinosaur*[57]

☐ *Danny and the Dinosaur: Too Tall*[58]

☐ *Charlie the Ranch Dog: Charlie's New Friend*[59]

☐ *The Berenstain Bears at the Aquarium*[60]

☐ *Blaze and the Gray Spotted Pony*[61]

☐ *Amelia Bedelia*[62]

☐ *Teach Us, Amelia Bedelia*[63]

☐ *Good Night, Good Knight*[64]

☐ *Amelia Bedelia Helps Out*[65]

☐ *Amelia Bedelia and the Baby*[66]

☐ *The Very Busy Spider*[67]

☐ *Mouse Soup*[68]

☐ *The Kitten Who Thought He Was a Mouse*[69]

☐ *The Poky Little Puppy*[70]

55. Gene Zion.
56. Gene Zion.
57. Syd Hoff.
58. Syd Hoff.
59. Ree Drummond.
60. Jan and Mike Berenstain.
61. C. W. Anderson.
62. Peggy Parish.
63. Peggy Parish.
64. Shelley Moore Thomas.
65. Peggy Parish.
66. Peggy Parish.
67. Eric Carle.
68. Arnold Lobel.
69. Miriam Norton. Little Golden Book.
70. Janette Sebring Lowrey. Little Golden Book.

☐ *Scuffy the Tugboat*[71]

☐ *The Please and Thank You Book*[72]

☐ *The Three Bears*[73]

☐ *Three Little Pigs*[74]

☐ *The Shy Little Kitten*[75]

☐ *How Do Penguins Play?*[76]

☐ *The Princess and the Pea*[77]

☐ *Mike Mulligan and His Steam Shovel*[78]

☐ *George the Drummer Boy*[79]

☐ *Strega Nona*[80]

☐ *The Selfish Giant*[81]

☐ *Lyle, Lyle, Crocodile*[82]

☐ *Buffalo Bill and the Pony Express*[83]

Level 3

☐ *Riding the Pony Express*[84]

☐ *The Bears on Hemlock Mountain*[85]

71. Gertrude Crampton. Little Golden Book.

72. Barbara Shook Hazen. Little Golden Book.

73. Feodor Rojankovsky. Little Golden Book.

74. R. H. Disney. Little Golden Book.

75. Cathleen Schurr. Little Golden Book.

76. Diane Muldrow. Little Golden Book.

77. Retelling of Hans Christian Andersen's story. Illustrated by Jana Christy. Little Golden Book.

78. Virginia Lee Burton.

79. Nathaniel Benchley.

80. Tomie de Paola. A Caldecott Honor book.

81. Oscar Wilde. Adaptation by Dan Goeller.

82. Bernard Waber.

83. Eleanor Coerr.

84. Clyde Robert Bulla.

85. Alice Dalgliesh. A Newbery Honor book.

- ☐ Childhood of Famous Americans series[86]
- ☐ *Uncle Wiggily's Storybook*[87]
- ☐ *Sarah, Plain and Tall*[88]
- ☐ *More About Paddington*[89]
- ☐ *A Bear Called Paddington*[90]
- ☐ *Paddington Helps Out*[91]
- ☐ *Paddington Goes to Town*[92]
- ☐ *Paddington at Work*[93]
- ☐ *Paddington at Large*[94]
- ☐ *Paddington Abroad*[95]
- ☐ *The Courage of Sarah Noble*[96]
- ☐ *The Boxcar Children*[97]
- ☐ *Encyclopedia Brown*[98]
- ☐ *The Cabin Faced West*[99]
- ☐ *Little House in the Big Woods*[100]
- ☐ *Little House on the Prairie*[101]

86. Aladdin Paperbacks.
87. Howard R. Garis.
88. Patricia MacLachlan. A Newbery Medal book.
89. Michael Bond.
90. Michael Bond.
91. Michael Bond.
92. Michael Bond.
93. Michael Bond.
94. Michael Bond.
95. Michael Bond.
96. Alice Dalgliesh. A Newbery Honor book.
97. Gertrude Chandler Warner.
98. Donald J. Sobol.
99. Jean Fritz.
100. Laura Ingalls Wilder.
101. Laura Ingalls Wilder.

☐ *Farmer Boy*[102]

☐ *On the Banks of Plum Creek*[103]

☐ *By the Shores of Silver Lake*[104]

☐ *The Long Winter*[105]

☐ *Little Town on the Prairie*[106]

☐ *These Happy Golden Years*[107]

☐ *The First Four Years*[108]

☐ The Milly-Molly-Mandy series[109]

☐ *In the Family*[110]

☐ *Pinocchio*[111]

☐ *The Railway Children*[112]

☐ *The Velveteen Rabbit*[113]

☐ Winnie-the-Pooh series: *Winnie-the-Pooh*[114]

☐ Winnie-the-Pooh series: *The House at Pooh Corner*[115]

☐ Winnie-the-Pooh series: *Return to the Hundred Acre Wood*[116]

☐ *Bo and the Missing Dogs*[117]

102. Laura Ingalls Wilder.
103. Laura Ingalls Wilder.
104. Laura Ingalls Wilder. A Newbery Honor book.
105. Laura Ingalls Wilder.
106. Laura Ingalls Wilder.
107. Laura Ingalls Wilder.
108. Laura Ingalls Wilder.
109. Joyce Lankester Brisley.
110. Farley Mowat.
111. Carlo Collodi.
112. E. Nesbit.
113. Margery Williams.
114. A.A. Milne.
115. A.A. Milne.
116. David Benedictus.
117. Lynn Sheffield Simmons.

- ☐ *The Adventures of Peter Cottontail and His Green Forest Friends*[118]
- ☐ *Bo, the Famous Retriever*[119]
- ☐ *Baby Island*[120]

Level 4

- ☐ *Pages of History* Vol. 1[121]
- ☐ *Pages of History* Vol. 2[122]
- ☐ *Book of Greek Myths*[123]
- ☐ *Alice in Wonderland* and *Through the Looking Glass*[124]
- ☐ *The Random House Book of Fairy Tales*[125]
- ☐ *Charlotte's Web*[126]
- ☐ *The Lion, the Witch and the Wardrobe*[127]
- ☐ *Prince Caspian*[128]
- ☐ *The Voyage of the Dawn Treader*[129]
- ☐ *The Silver Chair*[130]
- ☐ *The Horse and His Boy*[131]
- ☐ *The Magician's Nephew*[132]

118. Thornton W. Burgess.
119. Lynn Sheffield Simmons.
120. Carol Ryrie Brink.
121. Bruce Etter and Alexia Detwiler.
122. Bruce Etter and Alexia Detwiler.
123. Ingri and Edgar Parin d'Aulaire.
124. Lewis Carroll.
125. Adapted by Amy Ehrlich.
126. E. B. White. A Newbery Honor book.
127. C. S. Lewis.
128. C. S. Lewis.
129. C. S. Lewis.
130. C. S. Lewis.
131. C. S. Lewis.
132. C. S. Lewis.

☐ *The Last Battle*[133]

☐ *The Dragon of Lonely Island*[134]

☐ *The Return of the Dragon*[135]

☐ *Homer Price*[136]

☐ *Peter Pan*[137]

☐ *The Story of the Treasure Seekers*[138]

☐ *Stuart Little*[139]

☐ *A Little Princess*[140]

☐ *A Penny's Worth of Character*[141]

☐ *The Bronze Bow*[142]

☐ *The Light Princess, and Other Fairy Tales*[143]

☐ *The Princess and Curdie*[144]

☐ *The Princess and the Goblin*[145]

☐ *American Tall Tales*[146]

☐ *Hans Christian Anderson's Complete Fairy Tales*[147]

☐ *The Golden Key*[148]

133. C. S. Lewis.
134. Rebecca Rupp.
135. Rebecca Rupp.
136. Robert McCloskey.
137. J. M. Barrie.
138. E. Nesbit.
139. E. B. White.
140. Frances Hodgson Burnett.
141. Jesse Stuart.
142. Elizabeth George Speare. Newbery Medal Winner.
143. George MacDonald.
144. George MacDonald.
145. George MacDonald
146. Adrien Stoutenburg.
147. Translation by Jean Hersholt.
148. George MacDonald.

THE GOOD AND THE GREAT: BOOK *CHECKLIST* FOR KIDS

☐ *The White Dove*[149]

☐ *The Golden Thread*[150]

☐ *Tut's Mummy: Lost and Found*[151]

☐ *Cleopatra*[152]

☐ *Detectives in Togas*[153]

Level 5

☐ *Charlie and the Chocolate Factory*[154]

☐ *Faerie Gold: Treasures from the Lands of Enchantment*[155]

☐ *The Hobbit*[156]

☐ *Mary Poppins*[157]

☐ *Bound for Oregon*[158]

☐ *The Twenty-One Balloons*[159]

☐ *Rebecca of Sunnybrook Farm*[160]

☐ *Three Tales of My Father's Dragon*[161]

☐ *Little Women*[162]

☐ *Black Ships Before Troy: The Story of the Iliad*[163]

149. Christoph von Schmi.
150. Norman Macleod.
151. Judy Donnelly.
152. Diana Stanley and Peter Vennema.
153. Henry Winterfeld.
154. Roald Dahl.
155. Edited by Kathryn Lindskoog and Ranelda Mack Hunsicker.
156. J. R. R. Tolkien.
157. P. L. Travers.
158. Jean Van Leeuwen.
159. William Pene du Bois.
160. Kate Douglas Wiggin.
161. Ruth Stiles Gannett.
162. Louisa May Alcott.
163. Rosemary Sutcliff. Winner of the Cilip Kate Greenaway Medal.

- ☐ Aesop's Fables[164]
- ☐ *Hans Brinker, or The Silver Skates*[165]
- ☐ *Under the Lilacs*[166]
- ☐ *The Story of My Life*[167]
- ☐ *Wizard of Oz*[168]
- ☐ *An Old-Fashioned Girl*[169]
- ☐ *The Sign of the Beaver*[170]
- ☐ *Five Little Peppers and How They Grew*[171]
- ☐ Smith of Wootton Major[172]
- ☐ *Pecos Bill: The Greatest Cowboy of All Time*[173]
- ☐ *Children of the Covered Wagon*[174]
- ☐ *The Wind in the Willows*[175]
- ☐ *The Jumping Off Place*[176]
- ☐ *Luther the Leader*[177]
- ☐ *Girls of Courage Who Became Women of Influence*[178]
- ☐ *The Illusion*[179]

164. Illustrated by Arthur Rackham.
165. Mary Mapes Dodge.
166. Louisa May Alcott.
167. Helen Keller.
168. L. Frank Baum.
169. Louisa May Alcott.
170. Elizabeth George Speare. A Newbery Honor book.
171. Margaret Sidney.
172. J. R. R. Tolkien.
173. James Cloyd Bowman.
174. Mary Jane Carr.
175. Kenneth Grahame.
176. Marian Hurd McNeely. A Newbery Honor book.
177. Virgil Robinson.
178. Elsie E. Egermeier.
179. A. L. O. E. (pseudonym for Charlotte Maria Tucker). Lamplighter Collection.

☐ *Dangerous Journey: The Story of Pilgrim's Progress*[180]

☐ *Favorite Poems Old and New: Selected for Boys and Girls*[181]

Level 6

☐ *Heidi*[182]

☐ *The Swiss Family Robinson*[183]

☐ *The Secret Garden*[184]

☐ *Anne of Green Gables*[185]

☐ *Robinson Crusoe*[186]

☐ Lord of the Rings trilogy: *The Fellowship of the Ring*[187]

☐ Lord of the Rings trilogy: *The Two Towers*[188]

☐ Lord of the Rings trilogy: *The Return of the King*[189]

☐ Misty of Chincoteague series: *Misty of Chincoteague*[190]

☐ *Pollyanna*[191]

☐ *The Prince and the Pauper*[192]

☐ *Little Lord Fauntleroy*[193]

180. William B.

181. Selected by Helen Ferris. Illustrated by Leonard Weisgard. A *beautiful*, large book of mostly short poems. This is a selection of poems everyone should own, in my opinion. Exposes children to so many famous poets, and to a spellbinding collection of their works.

182. Johanna Spyri.

183. Johann David Wyss.

184. Frances Hodgson Burnett.

185. Lucy Maud Montgomery.

186. Daniel Defoe.

187. J. R. R. Tolkien.

188. J. R. R. Tolkien.

189. J. R. R. Tolkien.

190. Marguerite Henry. A Newbery Honor book.

191. Eleanor H. Porter.

192. Mark Twain.

193. Frances Hodgson Burnett.

☐ *Gulliver's Travels*[194]

☐ *Five Children and It*[195]

☐ *The Merry Adventures of Robin Hood*[196]

☐ *The Wyoming Ranch Letters: The Collected Correspondence of a Woman Settler on the American Frontier*[197]

☐ *The Door in the Wall*[198]

☐ *How John Norton Kept His Christmas*[199]

☐ *Father, M.P.*[200]

☐ *The Reluctant Dragon*[201]

☐ Misty of Chincoteague series[202]

☐ *Johnny Tremain*[203]

☐ *Mr. Bliss*[204]

Level 7

☐ *Monks and Mystics, Vol. 2: Chronicles of the Medieval Church*[205]

☐ *Mr. Pipes and Psalms and Hymns of the Reformation*[206]

☐ *The Accidental Voyage: Discovering Hymns of the Early Centuries*[207]

194. Jonathan Swift.
195. Edith Nesbit.
196. Howard Pyle.
197. Elinore Pruitt Stewart.
198. Marguerite Dr Angeli. A Newbery Award book.
199. W. H. H. Murray.
200. Theodora Wilson Wilson.
201. Kenneth Grahame.
202. Marguerite Henry.
203. Esther Forbes. Newbery Medal.
204. J. R. R. Tolkien.
205. Mindy and Brandon Withrow.
206. Douglas Bond.
207. Douglas Bond.

☐ *The Jungle Book*[208]

☐ *Farmer Giles of Ham*[209]

☐ *Once on This Island*[210]

☐ *The Children of the New Forest*[211]

☐ *At the Back of the North Wind*[212]

☐ *Captains Courageous*[213]

☐ *The Iliad and the Odyssey for Boys and Girls*[214]

☐ *The Light in the Forest*[215]

☐ *Seaman: The Dog Who Explored the West with Lewis & Clark*[216]

☐ *The Yearling*[217]

☐ *Squalls Before War: Her Majesty's Schooner Sultana*[218]

☐ *The Pilgrim's Progress*[219]

☐ *Kidnapped*[220]

☐ *A Christmas Carol*[221]

☐ *Through Gates of Splendor*[222]

☐ *Around the World in Eighty Days*[223]

208. Rudyard Kipling.
209. J. R. R. Tolkien.
210. Gloria Whelan.
211. Captain Marryat.
212. George MacDonald.
213. Rudyard Kipling.
214. Alfred Church.
215. Conrad Richter.
216. Gail Langer Karwoski.
217. Marjorie Kinnan Rawlings. Pulitzer Prize Winner.
218. Ned Bustard.
219. Paul Bunyan.
220. Robert Louis Stevenson.
221. Charles Dickens.
222. Elisabeth Elliot.
223. Jules Verne.

- ☐ *Macbeth*[224]
- ☐ *King Arthur and His Knights of the Round Table*[225]
- ☐ *Treasure Island*[226]
- ☐ *The One-Armed Sailor*[227]
- ☐ *My Life as an Indian*[228]
- ☐ *Kidnapped and Sold by Indians: True Story of a 7-Year-Old Settler Child*[229]
- ☐ *The Hobgoblins*[230]
- ☐ *Where the Red Fern Grows*[231]
- ☐ *Candy Bomber: The Story of the Berlin Airlift's "Chocolate Pilot"*[232]

Level 8

- ☐ *Mere Christianity*[233]
- ☐ *The Screwtape Letters*[234]
- ☐ *The Divine Comedy*[235]
- ☐ *Confessions*[236]
- ☐ *Eusebius: The Church History*[237]

224. William Shakespeare.
225. Roger Lancelyn Green.
226. Robert Louis Stevenson.
227. A. L. O. E. (pseudonym for Charlotte Maria Tucker).
228. James Willard Schultz.
229. Matthew Brayton.
230. Douglas Bond.
231. Wilson Rawls.
232. Michael O. Tunnell.
233. C. S. Lewis.
234. C. S. Lewis.
235. Dante Alighieri.
236. St. Augustine.
237. Translated by Paul L. Maier.

☐ *Beowulf*[238]

☐ *Sir Gawain and the Green Knight*[239]

☐ *The Black Arrow*[240]

☐ *Fahrenheit 451*[241]

☐ *The Great Divorce*[242]

☐ *My Captivity: A Pioneer Woman's Story of Her Life Among the Sioux*[243]

☐ *History, Law, and Christianity*[244]

☐ *Uncle Tom's Cabin*[245]

☐ *God's Double Agent: The True Story of a Chinese Christian's Fight for Freedom*[246]

☐ *The Odyssey of Homer*[247]

☐ *The Iliad of Homer*[248]

☐ *Republic*[249]

Additional "Just for Fun" Books & Series:

☐ Adventures of the Northwoods series[250]

☐ Christian Heroes: Then & Now series[251]

238. Translated by Seamus Heaney.
239. J. R. R. Tolkien.
240. Robert Louis Stevenson.
241. Ray Bradbury.
242. C. S. Lewis.
243. Fanny Kelly
244. Dr. John Warwick Montgomery
245. Harriet Beecher Stowe.
246. Bob Fu with Nancy French
247. Homer. Translated by Richard Lattimore.
248. Homer. Translated by Richard Lattimore.
249. Plato.
250. Louis Walfrid Johnson.
251. YWAM Publishing.

☐ The Viking Quest series[252]

☐ *The Mrs. Piggle Wiggle Treasury*[253]

☐ Winnie the Horse Gentler series[254]

☐ Nate the Great series[255]

☐ Billy and Blaze series[256]

☐ The Complete Flower Fairies books[257]

☐ The Oregon Trail series[258]

☐ Freedom Seekers series[259]

☐ *The Amazing Dr. Ransom's Bestiary of Adorable Fallacies: A Field Guide for Clear Thinkers*[260]

☐ Light Keepers Girls Box Set: Ten Girls[261]

☐ Faith and Freedom Trilogy[262]

☐ Crown and Covenant Series[263]

☐ The 1936 Nancy Drew Series[264]

☐ The 1927 Hardy Boys Mystery Series[265]

☐ The Complete Collection of Dr. Doolittle Stories[266]

☐ The Chronicles of Prydain series[267]

252. Lois Walfrid Johnson.
253. Betty MacDonald.
254. Dandi Daley Mackall.
255. Marjorie Weinman Sharmat.
256. C. W. Anderson.
257. Andrew Lang.
258. Jesse Wiley.
259. Lois Walfrid Johnson.
260. Douglas Wilson and N. D. Wilson.
261. Irene Howat
262. Douglas Bond.
263. Douglas Bond.
264. Carolyn Keene.
265. Franklin W. Dixon.
266. Hugh Lofting.
267. Alexander Lloyd.

- ☐ The New Junior Classics series[268]
- ☐ *Leepike Ridge*[269]
- ☐ *The Adventures of Geraldine Woolkins*[270]
- ☐ The Boxcar Children original series[271]
- ☐ The Roman Britain Trilogy[272]
- ☐ The Histories of Middle Earth series[273]
- ☐ *The Adventures of Tom Bombadil*[274]
- ☐ *Alone Yet Not Alone*[275]
- ☐ *A Sparrow Alone*[276]
- ☐ *Twice Freed*[277]
- ☐ *Adventure Lands*[278]
- ☐ *The Cat Who Wished to Be a Man*[279]
- ☐ The Space Trilogy[280]
- ☐ *Time Cat*[281]
- ☐ *The Town Cats & Other Tales*[282]
- ☐ *Flower Fables*[283]

268. 10 vols. 1953. Collier.
269. N. D. Wilson.
270. Karin Kaufman.
271. Gertrude Chandler Warner.
272. Rosemary Sutcliff.
273. J. R. R. Tolkien.
274. J. R. R. Tolkien.
275. Tracy Leininger Craven.
276. Alicia Petersen.
277. Patricia St. John.
278. Selected and edited by Leland B. Jacobs, Eleanor M. Johnson, and Jo Jasper Turner.
279. Lloyd Alexander.
280. C. S. Lewis.
281. Lloyd Alexander.
282. Lloyd Alexander.
283. Louisa May Alcott.

- [ ] *God King: A Story in the Days of King Hezekiah*[284]
- [ ] *Hittite Warrior*[285]
- [ ] *The Secret of the Ruby Ring*[286]
- [ ] *Mr. Popper's Penguins*[287]
- [ ] *Men of Iron*[288]
- [ ] Dog Diaries series[289]
- [ ] *Tirzah*[290]
- [ ] Sherlock Holmes mysteries[291]
- [ ] Lord Peter Wimsey mystery series[292]
- [ ] *Cathedral: The Story of Its Construction*[293]
- [ ] Tumtum and Nutmeg series[294]
- [ ] Lamplighter Collection books[295]
- [ ] The Happy Hollisters series[296]
- [ ] Dear America series[297]
- [ ] In Grandma's Attic series[298]
- [ ] *Cabin on Trouble Creek*[299]

284. Joanne Williamson.
285. Joanne Williamson.
286. Yvonne MacGrory.
287. Florence and Richard Atwater.
288. Howard Pyle.
289. Various authors. Published by Random House.
290. Lucille Travis.
291. Sir Arthur Conan Doyle.
292. Dorothy Sayers.
293. David Macaulay. A Caldecott Honor book.
294. Emily Bearn.
295. Lamplighter Ministries, publisher.
296. Jerry West.
297. Scholastic Books, publisher.
298. Arleta Richardson.
299. Jean van Leeuwen.

Bibliography

Alfonzo, Gina. *Dorothy and Jack: The Transforming Friendship of Dorothy L. Sayers and C. S. Lewis*. Grand Rapids: Baker, 1999.

American Academy of Child & Adolescent Psychiatry. "TV Violence and Children." December 2017. https://www.aacap.org/AACAP/Families_and_Youth/Facts_for_Families/FFF-Guide/Children-And-TV-Violence-013.aspx.

American College of Pediatricians. "Media Use and Screen Time—Its Impact on Children, Adolescents, and Families." May 2020. https://acpeds.org/position-statements/media-use-and-screen-time-its-impact-on-children-adolescents-and-families.

Augustine. *City of God*. Translated by Marcus Dods. New York: Modern Library, 1950. https://www.logoslibrary.org/augustine/city/1522.html.

Berns, Gregory S., et al., "Short- and Long-Term Effects of a Novel on Connectivity in the Brain." *Brain Connectivity* 3.6 (2013) 590–600. https://doi.org/10.1089/brain.2013.0166.

Buck, Daniel. "Horace Mann's Solution to Political Turmoil in Education." Thomas B. Fordham Institute, February 22, 2024. https://fordhaminstitute.org/national/commentary/horace-manns-solution-political-turmoil-education.

Burge, Dave. "Fight at Socorro ISD School Going Viral on Social Media." KTSM 9 News, May 20, 2024. https://www.ktsm.com/news/fight-at-socorro-isd-school-going-viral-on-social-media/.

Cambridge Dictionary. "Focus." https://dictionary.cambridge.org/us/dictionary/english/focus.

———. "Self-Discipline." https://dictionary.cambridge.org/us/dictionary/english/self-discipline.

Cheema, Kulpreet, and Jacqueline Cummine. "The Relationship Between White Matter and Reading Acquisition, Refinement and Maintenance." *Developmental Neuroscience* 40.3 (2018) 209–22. https://doi.org/10.1159/000489491.

Dewey, John. *Democracy and Education*. Ebook. Unversity Park, PA: The Pennsylvania State University, 2001. https://nsee.memberclicks.net/assets/docs/KnowledgeCenter/BuildingExpEduc/BooksReports/10.%20democracy%20and%20education%20by%20dewey.pdf.

Dobson, James. *The New Strong-Willed Child*. 4th ed. Carol Stream, IL: Tyndale House, 1952.

Eleanorfan1111. "The Last Interview With Grace Kelly—on ABC's 20/20 (Part 3 of 6)." YouTube, May 31, 2009, 04:41–05:50. https://www.youtube.com/watch?v=pKAo jm7QG80.

Engelman, Siegfried, et al. *Teach Your Child to Read in 100 Easy Lessons*. New York: Simon & Schuster, 1986.

Flexner, James T. *George Washington*. 1st ed. Boston, MA: Little, Brown and Company, 1967.

Forbes, Thomas A., and Vittorio Gallo. "All Wrapped Up: Environmental Effects on Myelination." *Trends in Neurosciences* 40.9 (2017) 572–87. https://doi.org/ 10.1016/j. tins.2017.06.009.

Foulkes, Lucy, et al. "Age Differences in the Prosocial Influence Effect." *Developmental Science* 21.6 (2018). https://doi.org/10.1111/desc.12666.

Hannah, Kristin. *The Women*. New York: St. Martin's, 2024.

Hutton, John S., et al. "Associations Between Home Literacy Environment, Brain White Matter Integrity and Cognitive Abilities in Preschool-Age Children." *Acta Paediatrica* 109.7 (2019) 1376–86. https://pmc.ncbi.nlm.nih.gov/articles/PMC7318131/.

———. "Associations Between Screen-Based Media Use and Brain White Matter Integrity in Preschool-Aged Children." *JAMA Pediatrics* 174.1 (2019) e193869. https://pmc. ncbi.nlm.nih.gov/articles/PMC6830442/.

Indy Parenting Staff. "Education Reimagined at Santa Barbara Free School." *The Santa Barbara Independent*, July 24, 2023. https://www.independent.com/2023/07/24/ education-reimagined-at-santa-barbara-free-school/.

Jones, Charlie. "California Teen, 14, Takes Own Life After Vile School Bullying for Being Homeless and Having No Mom." The Mirror US, November 14, 2024. https://www. themirror.com/news/us-news/california-teen-14-takes-life-805522.

Jones, Jeffrey M. "LGBTQ+ Identification in U.S. Now at 7.6%." Gallup, March 13, 2024. https://news.gallup.com/poll/611864/lgbtq-identification.aspx.

Kopff, Christian. "Greek to Us: The Death of Classical Education & Its Consequences." The Imaginative Conservative, July 26, 2023. https://theimaginativeconservative. org/2023/07/death-classical-education-christian-kopff.html.

Kozakiewicz, Alicia. "Kidnapped by a Paedophile I Met Online." BBC News, March 7, 2016. https://www.bbc.com/news/magazine-35730298.

Kreide, Anita Therese. "Literacy Achievement in Nongraded Classrooms." PhD diss., Loyola Marymount University, 2016. https://digitalcommons.lmu.edu/cgi/view content.cgi?article=1193&context=etd.

Ladson-Billings, Gloria. "From the Achievement Gap to the Education Debt: Understanding Achievement in U.S. Schools." *Educational Researcher* 35.7 (2006) 3–12. https://www.jstor.org/stable/3876731.

Lee, Amber. "14-year-old Dies by Suicide After Santa Clara Schoolmates Bully Him About Being Homeless: Father." Fox 2 KTVU, November 12, 2024. https://www.ktvu.com/ news/14-year-old-dies-suicide-after-santa-clara-schoolmates-bully-him-about-being-homeless-father.

Lencki, Maria. "Vivek Ramaswamy Exposes 'National Security Risk' as Students Fall Behind in School." Fox News, February 1, 2025. https://www.foxnews.com/media/ vivek-ramaswamy-exposes-national-security-risk-students-fall-behind-school.

Lewis, C. S. *The Screwtape Letters*. New York: HarperOne, 1996.

Lissak, Gadi. "Adverse Physiological and Psychological Effects of Screen Time on Children and Adolescents: Literature Review and Case Study." *Environmental Research* 164 (2018) 149–57. https://doi.org/10.1016/j.envres.2018.01.015.

Loveliveserve. "Asking College Students Basic Questions (THEY FAILED MISERABLY . . . .)." YouTube, March 26, 2022. https://www.youtube.com/watch?v=cV0AgB88JE4.

McDonald, George. "Marion Woman Raises Safety Concerns Following School Fight." WAKA 8, August 30, 2024. https://www.waka.com/2024/08/29/marion-woman-raises-safety-concerns-following-school-fight/.

Moore, Michele J., et al. "Sexual Behaviors of Middle School Students: 2009 Youth Risk Behaviors Survey Results from 16 Locations." *Journal of School Health* 83.1 (2013) 61–68. https://doi.org/10.1111/j.1746-1561.2012.00748.x.

Moulton, Gary E, ed. *Meriwether Lewis and William Clark: The Definitive Journals of Lewis and Clark.* 13 vols. University of Nebraska, 1991.

Moyer, Melinda Wenner. "Kids as Young as 8 Are Using Social Media More Than Ever, Study Finds." *The New York Times*, March 24, 2022. https://www.nytimes.com/2022/03/24/well/family/child-social-media-use.html.

The Nation's Report Card. "National Achievement-Level Results." https://www.nationsreportcard.gov/mathematics/nation/achievement/?grade=12.

National Literacy Institute. "Literacy Statistics 2022–2023." https://www.thenationalliteracyinstitute.com/post/literacy-statistics-2022-2023.

———. "Literacy Statistics 2024–2025 (Where We Are Now)." https://www.thenationalliteracyinstitute.com/post/literacy-statistics-2024-2025-where-we-are-now#:~:text=54%25%20of%20adults%20have%20a,highest%20rate%20of%20child%20literacy.

National Park Service. "Antietam: Letters and Diaries of Soldiers and Civilians." https://www.nps.gov/anti/learn/education/classrooms/antietam-letters-and-diaries-of-soldiers-and-civilians.htm?ms=googlegrant.

Nietzsche, Friedrich. *The Joyful Wisdom: La Gaya Scienza.* Translated by Thomas Common. Edinburgh: T. N. Foulis, 1910.

Noozhawk. "Santa Barbara Free School's Mission Is to Create a Vibrant Community That Grows for Generations." October 24, 2023. https://www.noozhawk.com/santa-barbara-frees-mission-is-to-create-a-vibrant-school-community-that-grows-for-generations/.

O'Niell, Brian. "The Influence of Social Media on the Development of Children and Young People." European Parliament, February 2023. https://www.europarl.europa.eu/RegData/etudes/STUD/2023/733109/IPOL_STU(2023)733109_EN.pdf.

Oxford Learner's Dictionaries. "Socialization." https://www.oxfordlearnersdictionaries.com/us/definition/english/socialization.

Pace, David. "Parents Speak Out After 16-year-old Is Viciously Beaten in School Hallway as Students Film Attack." East Idaho News, December 2, 2024. https://www.eastidahonews.com/2024/10/parents-speak-out-after-16-year-old-is-viciously-beaten-in-school-hallway-as-students-film-attack/.

Pew Research Center. "Teens, Video Games and Civics." September 16, 2008. https://www.pewresearch.org/internet/2008/09/16/teens-video-games-and-civics/.

Ponti, Michelle, et al. "Screen Time and Young Children: Promoting Health and Development in a Digital World." *Paediatrics & Child Health* 22.8 (2017) 461–68. https://pubmed.ncbi.nlm.nih.gov/29601064/.

Purves, D., et al. "Increased Conduction Velocity as a Result of Myelination." In *Neuroscience*. 2nd ed. Sunderland, MA: Sinauer Associates, 2001. https://www.ncbi.nlm.nih.gov/books/NBK10921/.

Reissler, Irina. "Media Violence and Its Impact on Society and Teenagers." MA thesis, California State University, Monterey Bay, 2006. https://digitalcommons.csumb.edu/cgi/viewcontent.cgi?article=1018&context=caps_thes.

Sager, Jeanne. "Diving into 2024 NAEP Reading Test Results—What Every Educator Needs to Know." Ignite Reading, January 29, 2025. https://ignite-reading.com/naep-reading-test-results/.

Santos, Renata Maria Silva, et al. "The Association Between Screen Time and Attention in Children: A Systematic Review." *Developmental Neuropsychology* 47.4 (2022) 175–92. https://doi.org/10.1080/87565641.2022.2064863.

Sayers, Dorothy. *The Lost Tools of Learning: Symposium on Education*. Ireland: CrossReach, 2014.

Schaffer, Katherine. "Among Many U.S. Children, Reading for Fun Has Become Less Common, Federal Data Shows." Pew Research Center, November 21, 2021. https://www.pewresearch.org/short-reads/2021/11/12/among-many-u-s-children-reading-for-fun-has-become-less-common-federal-data-shows/.

———. "U.S. Public, Private and Charter Schools in 5 Charts." Pew Research Center, June 6, 2024. https://www.pewresearch.org/short-reads/2024/06/06/us-public-private-and-charter-schools-in-5-charts/.

Silver, Caleb. "The Top 25 Economies in the World." Investopedia, January 29, 2025. https://www.investopedia.com/insights/worlds-top-economies/.

Sparks, Sarah D. "Two Decades of Progress, Nearly Gone: National Math, Reading Scores Hit Historic Lows." *Education Week*, October 24, 2022. https://www.edweek.org/leadership/two-decades-of-progress-nearly-gone-national-math-reading-scores-hit-historic-lows/2022/10.

Statista. "Digital Advertising: Market Data & Analysis." https://www.statista.com/study/42540/digital-advertising-report/.

———. "Revenue in the Advertising Market United States 2020–2030." April 15, 2025. https://www.statista.com/forecasts/1435654/revenue-advertising-advertising-market-united-states.

Stone, Shomari. "Brutal School Assault Caught on Video: Parents Demand Justice for Maryland Teen." Fox 5 Washington DC, December 10, 2024. https://www.fox5dc.com/news/brutal-school-assault-caught-video-parents-demand-justice-maryland-teen.

Strasburger, Victor C. "Children, Adolescents, and Advertising," *Pediatrics* 118.6 (2006) 2563–69. https://doi.org/10.1542/peds.2006-2698.

Suggate, Sebastian Paul. "Does It Kill the Imagination Dead? The Effect of Film Versus Reading on Mental Imagery." *American Psychological Association* (2023). https://doi.org/10.1037/aca0000651.

Treisman, Rachel. "The Wisconsin Shooting Suspect Is Female. That's Rare, Data Says." NPR, December 17, 2024. https://www.npr.org/2024/12/17/nx-s1-5231532/wisconsin-school-shooting-suspect-female.

Zouves, Natasha, and Hannah Follman. "Indiana 10-year-old Dies by Suicide After Being Targeted Bullies." News Nation, May 17, 2024. https://www.newsnationnow.com/us-news/education/indiana-10-year-old-dies-by-suicide-bullying/.

www.ingramcontent.com/pod-product-compliance
Lightning Source LLC
Chambersburg PA
CBHW070919270326
41927CB00011B/2641